MARIJUANA LAW

MARIJUANA
LAW

by Richard Glen Boire
Attorney at Law

Ronin Publishing, Inc.   Box 1035   Berkeley CA 94701

Marijuana Law
ISBN: 0-914171-62-3
Copyright © 1992 by Richard Glen Boire

Published by
Ronin Publishing, Inc.
Post Office Box 1035
Berkeley, California 94701

Printed in the United States of America
First Edition 1993

9 8 7 6 5 4

Project Editors: Sebastian Orfali, Beverly Potter
Manuscript Editors: Aiden Kelly, Sebastian Orfali
Layout and Design: William Capps III, Ginger Ashworth
Index: Nancy Freedom
Cover: Brian Groppe

U.S. Library of Congress Cataloging in Publication Data
Boire, Richard Glen, 1964 –
          Marijuana law / by Richard Glen Boire.
                    p.   cm.
          Includes index.
          ISBN 0-914171-62-3 : $12.95
          1. Marijuana—Law and legislation—United States—Popular works.
2. Criminal procedure—United States—Popular works.   I. Title.
KF3891.M2B65 1993
345.73 ' 0277—dc20
[347.305277]   93–192
                                                                        CIP

DEDICATION

For all my relations.

ACKNOWLEDGMENT

I would like to thank my wife Sharon, without whom this book would have been impossible. I would also like to thank my friends and colleagues who read early drafts of the manuscript and provided valuable suggestions and invaluable encouragement, particularly, my good friend, Leslie Bialick, Attorney at Law.

Foreword

by J. Tony Serra, Attorney at Law

WE marijuana smokers in the United States are an oppressed category of citizen. We are tracked down like animals, mostly by secret police, treated brutally, ripped off by lawyers, and ultimately physically broken by unfair law and bad judges. We are being savaged by the legal system. Basic constitutional rights are denied to us. Harsh and inequitable jail sentences make martyrs of us all. Law and law enforcement have targeted us for extinction.

We are also victims of false law-enforcement propaganda about marijuana. We know the truth: that all of the evidence shows that marijuana is good for people; first as medicine and more meaningfully as a consciousness enhancer. Why should we be sacrificed to governmental falsity alleging negative attributes of marijuana use?

A government that knowingly issues false dogmas concerning marijuana and then through its laws ruthlessly crushes marijuana users, must be resisted and defied at the same level that it threatens us. That level is the legal-judicial realm. We must be armed in that realm in order to preserve ourselves. We must be armed with the "law."

Richard Boire's *Marijuana Law* gives us the legal armaments with which to resist unfair police methods. His book contains the most important things about marijuana law that a user must know. It is like our self-defense manual to guide us to freedom through the maze of onerous anti-marijuana laws.

The author lays out all the marijuana law in the field for us: arrest, search and seizure, court procedures, sentencing, fourth-amendment rights, drug testing, etc. His work is articulate and complete. If we are to survive we all must read and learn these principles. They connect directly with our freedom and ultimate ability to overthrow these unfair laws.

I urge every marijuana smoker to turn Richard Boire's book *Marijuana Law* into usable knowledge. We must know the law to fight the law. We must fight fire with fire. We must know the law to resist and defy injustice.

Table of Contents

Prologue

A<small>T</small> the outset, I should express my intentions in conveying the information herein. First, a review of recent decisions by the United States Supreme Court makes painfully clear that the constitutional rights guaranteeing some of our most cherished freedoms are being drastically narrowed. Moreover, in many cases the Court has rationalized its decision, in part, due to the need to combat the "War on Drugs." This book is intended to document some of the rights we are losing under the guise of fighting the "War on Drugs." Primarily, however, this book is written in the hopes that people will begin to stridently exercise and protect what constitutional protections remain.

Second, our country was founded on the principle of individual liberty and freedom. Does that not presuppose the right of each individual, at the very least, to retain control over his body and his mind? Is not the primary right in a free society the right of each individual to do with his body and his mind as he thinks best—provided no injury comes to others? What freedom remains when one loses the right to be the sole controller of his mind and body?

It is my belief that the current laws making criminal the possession and personal use of natural plants such as Cannabis, are unjust and contrary to the most fundamental of human freedoms. I perceive the government's banning of Cannabis as not one whit different than the government's banning of a particular book. I will read the books *I* choose regardless of the government's proscriptions. I will hold the thoughts *I* believe are just and true, regardless of the government's attempts to limit them. Likewise, *I alone*, shall decide how to manage my consciousness. My mind is my own.

Introduction

"If a nation expects to be ignorant and free, it expects what never was and never will be.... The people cannot be safe without information. Where the press is free, and every man able to read, all is safe."

Thomas Jefferson

Currently, over 30 million people in the United States regularly smoke marijuana. Many smoke to unwind after a busy day, to relieve stress, or simply for fun. Some smoke for spiritual reasons such as to assist in meditation, to be more conscious of the present, or to peak their awareness at all levels. Others, suffering from AIDS, cancer, chronic pain, glaucoma, and stomach ailments, smoke marijuana because they find it to be the most effective, safe, and least costly treatment for their condition.

Despite the fact that the vast majority of marijuana smokers are otherwise law-abiding and productive citizens, the federal government, as well as every state, has chosen to make even the possession of marijuana a crime, and has vowed to fight the "War on Drugs." As a result, in the average year, 400,000 people are arrested on some type of marijuana crime.

Perhaps recognizing the impact of the war on individual liberties, the war's leader has officially been labeled the "Drug Czar." The Czar's field commanders in the war are agents of the Drug Enforcement Administration and various state law-enforcement agencies. Indicative of the commanders' vilification of marijuana, and those who smoke it, is a statement made by outgoing Los Angeles Chief of Police, Daryl Gates, who in testimony before the Senate Judiciary Committee, stated that he favored the death penalty for even casual users of marijuana!

Fortunately, because our nation's founders rebelled against a government they perceived as tyrannical, they had the foresight to create the Bill of Rights. Those first ten amendments to the Constitution (especially the Fourth, Fifth, and Sixth Amendments) protect citizens in the United States from overzealous government officials such as Mr. Gates.

Unfortunately, caught up in the fervor of their misguided attempt to win the war on drugs, police and drug agents consistently trample the Bill of Rights whenever it gets in their way. Their blatant disregard for the Bill of Rights often goes unresisted because citizens are ignorant of their rights and therefore fail to assert them.

As the introductory quote by Thomas Jefferson so eloquently states, citizens must be informed of their rights in order to preserve them and remain free. Simply put, the purpose of this book is to inform marijuana users of their rights and how to protect and assert them.

This book is based on federal law (both constitutional and statutory) as well as state law. The federal law is applicable to all people in the U.S. regardless of their state of residence. The state law discussed will likewise be applicable to just about every reader, regardless of his or her state of residence. Forty-eight states, as well as the District of Columbia, have adopted the same basic anti-drug laws known as the Uniform Controlled Substances Act or the Uniform Narcotic Drug Act. In these states, the laws are generally identical except with respect to sentencing. The only two states that have not adopted the U.C.S.A. or U.N.D.A. are New Hampshire and Vermont; however, the law in those states is nearly identical to that in all the others, and of course federal law is fully applicable.

After reading this book, you will be armed with a thorough understanding of your legal rights in general and specifically with regard to marijuana. An emphasis will be placed on protections under the United States Constitution. For example, you will learn: when a police officer can legally stop you, when he can search you, when you have to be read your rights, what to do if an officer comes to your home with a search warrant, and how to counter many questionable police tactics by simply knowing and asserting your rights.

Many of the examples in this book are taken from actual court cases. Occasional factual changes have been made to help illustrate particular principles.

As a final comment, I should note that although this book was written in the early part of 1992, the law is always changing. Therefore, if you retain a lawyer to defend you on a marijuana charge you should follow his or her advice whenever it conflicts with this book.

Best of Luck. RGB

1. Crimes & Punishment

As you will understand after reading this book, the laws regarding marijuana are very similar to the rules of a board game such as "Monopoly." Like Monopoly, the better you know the rules, the more likely you'll be able to use the rules to your advantage and hopefully win the game. Unlike Monopoly however, the marijuana game is for real. If you lose, you pay real fines with real money and spend real days behind real jail bars.

Just about any activity involving the Cannabis plant is a criminal offense. For example, in every state it is an offense to possess marijuana, transport marijuana, drive under the influence of marijuana, sell marijuana, and grow marijuana. As an introduction to the laws concerning marijuana, this chapter will begin with several definitions and then move on to discuss the various marijuana crimes, their associated punishments, and the laws concerning forfeiture.

"Marijuana" Defined

UNDER federal and state statutory law, "marijuana" is commonly defined as "all parts of the plant *Cannabis sativa L.*, whether growing or not." This includes the seeds, resin and any derivatives, mixtures, or preparations of the plant. The federal definition, as well as those of most states, exclude the "mature stalks" of the plant as well as the sterilized seeds. The state of California's legal definition of marijuana is typical. It states in full:

> "Marijuana" means all parts of the plant *Cannabis sativa L.*, whether growing or not; the seeds thereof; the resin extracted from any part of the plant; and every compound, manufacture, salt, derivative, mixture, or preparation of the plant, its seeds or resin. It does not include the mature stalks of the plant, fiber produced from the stalks, oil or cake made from the seeds of the plant, any other compound, manufacture, salt, derivative, mixture, or preparation of the mature stalks (except the resin

extracted therefrom), fiber, oil, or cake, or the sterilized seed of the plant which is incapable of germination.

As the courts quickly learned, marijuana users were often more sophisticated than the legislators who wrote the legal definition of "marijuana." In several court cases, users charged with possession of marijuana argued that they possessed the species *Cannabis indica*, not *Cannabis sativa*, and that the law, by its own terms, only outlawed *Cannabis sativa*.

Faced with such arguments, the courts of all states have broadly interpreted the definition of "marijuana" to include all species of Cannabis that contain the active ingredient delta-9-tetrahydrocannabinol (THC). Therefore, although many statutory definitions of marijuana only mention *Cannabis sativa*, all species of marijuana containing THC, including *Cannabis indica* and *Cannabis ruderalis*, are outlawed. Some states, such as New York, have avoided the entire problem by outlawing "all plants of the genus Cannabis."

"Concentrated Cannabis" Defined

In addition to defining "marijuana," most states carve out a subsection of Cannabis preparations termed "concentrated Cannabis." Concentrated Cannabis is usually defined as the separated resins obtained from Cannabis. For example, hash oil is legally classified as concentrated Cannabis rather than marijuana. As will be seen later in this chapter, crimes involving concentrated Cannabis are punished more severely than identical crimes involving marijuana.

Synthetic Equivalents

In addition to the Cannabis plant, and its natural by-products, federal and state laws have criminalized the possession of all synthetic equivalents of the substances contained in the Cannabis plant. These human-made substances are usually referred to by the legal term "tetrahydrocannabinols."

The Burden of Proof

"It is better that twelve guilty men go free than that one innocent man be convicted."

Let's face it, being convicted of a criminal offense can really mess up your life. Not only are you branded by society as a criminal, but you also can be sent to prison, fined enormous amounts of money, and for some crimes, even executed. Given such serious consequences of a criminal conviction, our legal system requires a high level of proof in order to convict a person of a crime. This level of proof is known as "beyond a reasonable doubt."

In theory, a judge or jury can only convict a person of a marijuana crime if it finds, beyond a reasonable doubt, that the person committed each and every element of the crime charged. (As will be explained in the following sections, all crimes are composed of "elements," and each must be proven in order to be found guilty of the crime.) In other words, if the judge or jury has a doubt concerning one of the elements of the crime charged, and that doubt is reasonable, they (theoretically) should *not* find the person guilty of the crime charged. (In that case the person would be declared "not guilty." There is no verdict of "innocent" in our legal system.)

The definition of a "reasonable doubt" is explained in the instruction that the jury hears before it enters the jury room to decide upon its verdict. In California, for example, the jury is instructed:

> A defendant in a criminal action is presumed to be innocent until the contrary is proved, and in case of a reasonable doubt whether [his] guilt is satisfactorily shown, [he] is entitled to a verdict of not guilty. This presumption places upon the People the burden of proving [him] guilty beyond a reasonable doubt.

> Reasonable doubt is defined as follows: It is not a mere possible doubt; because everything relating to human affairs, and depending on moral evidence, is open to some possible or imaginary doubt. It is that state of the case which, after the entire comparison and consideration of all the evidence, leaves the minds of the jurors in that condition that they cannot say they feel an abiding conviction, to a moral certainty, of the truth of the charge.

A good example of the stringency of the "beyond a reasonable doubt" standard is given by the Illinois case of Ms. Jackson. One day, Ms. Jackson was in her apartment when she heard a knock at her front door. When she opened the door she was greeted by several police officers with a search warrant. Ms. Jackson, who happened to be carrying her purse at the time, stepped aside to allow the officers to enter. Then, without warning, she darted into her bathroom and locked the bathroom door.

One of the officers ran after her, pounded on the bathroom door and ordered her to open it. After a short hesitation, Ms. Jackson opened the door and was quickly handcuffed.

The officers searched her home pursuant to the search warrant but were unable to find any marijuana. However, as they searched the bathroom, one officer noticed that the bathtub appeared to have fresh footprints on its rim directly below an open window high on the wall. Suspecting that Ms. Jackson stood on the tub and tossed her marijuana out the window, the officer ran downstairs to see what he could find. Just as he suspected, among the debris below Ms. Jackson's bathroom window, he found a baggie containing marijuana. In addition, the baggie was dry whereas all the other debris in the area was wet from some earlier rains. All the evidence seemed to show that the marijuana had been tossed out of the bathroom window by Ms. Jackson.

When Ms. Jackson's case went to trial, her lawyer attempted to raise a reasonable doubt in the minds of the jury. He pointed out that as many as seven other apartments had windows located above the area where the marijuana-filled baggie was found. Additionally, he noted that it had not rained for two days, and hence, the baggie could have been deposited on the ground any time within the two days preceding Ms. Jackson's arrest.

Although the jury rejected her lawyer's arguments and convicted Ms. Jackson for possession of the marijuana, the conviction was reversed on appeal. The appellate court reversed her conviction after determining that, given the facts, it was impossible for a juror not to have a reasonable doubt that Ms. Jackson ever possessed the marijuana. The officers never saw her with the baggie, and hence the jury could not possibly have found she actually possessed the baggie. Likewise, (as will be explained later in this chapter) because the marijuana was not found inside her apartment, but rather outside, in a public place, the jury could not have found that she exercised dominion and control over the marijuana. Therefore, the appellate court reversed Ms. Jackson's conviction, finding that a doubt did exist and that such a doubt was at least reasonable.

The Crime of Possessing Marijuana

UNDER federal law and the laws of every state, it is a crime to possess marijuana. In order to convict a person of possession, most states require that the prosecution prove three things (known as "elements" of the crime). First, that the person on trial was caught possessing "a usable amount" of marijuana. Second, that the person "possessed" the marijuana. Lastly, that the person knew that he or she possessed an illegal drug. If the prosecution fails to prove even one of these elements, the person should be found *not guilty* of possessing marijuana.

A jury deciding a marijuana case is informed of the above elements and told it must find each element has been proven beyond a reasonable doubt in order to return a conviction for possessing marijuana. After all the evidence in the case has been presented, the jury is informed of the three elements by the judge who instructs them on the law. The actual jury instruction read to California juries in a marijuana-possession case is as follows:

> The defendant is accused of having committed the crime of illegal possession of a controlled substance, in violation of the Health and Safety Code.
>
> Every person who possesses a controlled substance, namely, marijuana, is guilty of the crime of illegal possession of a controlled substance. In order to prove such crime, each of the following elements must be proved:
>
> 1. The defendant exercised control or the right to control marijuana,
> 2. The defendant had knowledge of its presence,
> 3. The defendant had knowledge of its nature as a controlled substance, and
> 4. The substance was in an amount sufficient to be used as a controlled substance.

To expand on the above, the first thing the prosecution must prove is the element of possession. This can be proved in two ways. First, the prosecutor will try and show that the person had actual physical possession of the marijuana; for example, holding a joint in his hands, lips, or pocket. If the prosecutor is unable to prove that the person actually held the marijuana, he will try and show that the marijuana was within the person's "dominion and control." Often this is done by showing that the marijuana was found in an area or container that was under the person's control, for example, in the person's house, car, or backpack. The California jury instruction regarding these two types of possession states:

> Actual possession requires that a person knowingly exercise direct physical control over a thing.
>
> Constructive possession does not require actual possession but does require that a person knowingly exercise control or the right to control a thing, either directly or through another person or persons.

In one case in Texas, police discovered marijuana in two locked chests inside of a vehicle's trunk. Mr. Martinez was convicted of possessing the marijuana despite the fact that he neither owned the vehicle nor had ever driven the vehicle. The court held that Mr. Martinez was guilty of constructively possessing the marijuana because he was found with keys that unlocked the vehicle's trunk and the two chests containing the marijuana.

The case of Ms. Jackson, described earlier, is a good example of how difficult it is to convict a person of possessing marijuana that is found in a public place, and not in actual possession of any person. The courts of all states have ruled that a person's mere proximity to marijuana found in public is insufficient, standing alone, to convict the person of possessing the marijuana. The case of Monty is a common example of this rule in operation.

Officers Jones and Smith were assigned to handle drug detail at a local concert. Both officers were in uniform and simply walked among the concert-goers looking for people smoking pot, and hoping that their uniformed presence would deter people from smoking. As the officers walked down an aisle, Officer Jones observed a baggie of "green vegetable matter" on the ground near the feet of Monty, an eighteen-year-old concert-goer, wearing a Grateful Dead shirt. Officer Jones quickly grabbed the baggie, and by smell, tentatively identified it as containing marijuana. The officers grabbed Monty, who was seated directly above the baggie.

Monty's lawyer argued that there was insufficient evidence to convict Monty of possessing the marijuana since, other than the fact that Monty was the person closest to the marijuana, there was no evidence that Monty had dominion and control over it. Monty admitted that he knew what marijuana was, but denied that the marijuana that the officer's found was his.

The court that heard Monty's case agreed that Monty could not be convicted without more evidence linking him to the marijuana. The court explained that the crucial fact was that the marijuana was found on public property and could have been dropped by any one of the 6,000 concert fans. Because the officers never saw Monty actually holding the baggie or tossing it to the ground, there was no proof that he had dominion and control over the marijuana, and therefore he could not be convicted of possession.

In addition to proving that the person possessed the marijuana (actually or constructively), the prosecutor must prove that the person had knowledge that the item possessed was marijuana or some other unlawful substance. Since the prosecutor cannot get inside the person's head, he is often unable to prove *actual knowledge.* Therefore, the knowledge element is generally proved circumstantially. This means the prosecutor will try and prove, based on the person's behavior before or after he was arrested, that he knew the substance was marijuana (e.g., the person tried to hide the marijuana, or gave evasive answers when questioned by the police officer). Almost anything that shows the jury that the person knew what marijuana is, can, and will, be used to prove the knowledge element.

Most courts require very little proof of knowledge. The reality is that when a person is caught in possession of marijuana, the courts come very close to just assuming that the person was very much aware that the substance they possessed was marijuana or some other illegal drug.

Lastly, in addition to possession and knowledge, the prosecution must prove that the person was caught with a usable amount of marijuana—in other words, an amount of marijuana that could be rolled into a joint or smoked in a pipe by the average person. Therefore, if a person is found with only a few flakes of marijuana, a prosecutor will be unable to convict the person of possession.

It is important to understand that this is a test of quantity not quality. The prosecutor simply has to prove that the amount of marijuana possessed was enough to use. The prosecutor does not have to prove that the amount would in fact produce an effect. In other words, you can not argue that your marijuana was so impotent that the joint or bag of leaves that the cop found could not produce an effect. That is an argument of quality rather than quantity and would be considered irrelevant in court.

Although the law in most states requires that the prosecutor prove a usable amount, be advised that there is a recent trend in some states to uphold possession convictions where there was a sufficient quantity of the drug to permit *identification*, even though it was not a sufficient quantity for use. If this trend takes hold, the possession of even a minute amount of marijuana could be sufficient for a possession conviction since with today's high-technology laboratory procedures, only a very small quantity is needed for identification.

Punishment for Possessing Marijuana

SENTENCING for marijuana crimes varies from state to state. Currently, the most lenient states are California, Colorado, Maine, Massachusetts, Minnesota, Mississippi, North Carolina, Nebraska, New York, Ohio, and Oregon. In those states, conviction of possessing a small amount (usually less than an ounce) will result in a fine, but no jail time. Regardless of which state you live in, the sentence for possessing marijuana depends on several factors, including: how much marijuana was found, how old you were when arrested, how many prior convictions you have, and the type of property you were on when arrested. Needless to say, all these factors can make sentencing rather complex.

For example, in California, when determining the sentence for marijuana possession, the magic number is 28.5 grams (about an ounce). Regardless of your age, if you are convicted in California of possessing 28.5 grams or less of marijuana, you are fined approximately $100 and the conviction goes on your record as a misdemeanor. (A misdemeanor is less serious than a felony.) Moreover, you do not spend any time in jail.

The punishment for possessing marijuana gets a bit harsher if you were arrested on the grounds of an elementary, junior high, or high school, when a school activity was in session. In such a case, if you possessed 28.5 grams or less, you will be fined a maximum of $500 and/or sentenced to 10 days in county jail. However, if you are under 18 when arrested, then upon conviction you will be fined a maximum of $250, unless you have 2 or more prior convictions, in which case you can be fined $500 and/or placed in juvenile hall for 10 days.

If you are convicted of possessing more than 28.5 grams of marijuana, then regardless of your age or where you were arrested, you will be fined a maximum of $500 and/or sentenced to 6 months in county jail. Lastly, possession of any amount of Concentrated Cannabis can be punished by a maximum fine of $500 and/or a one year sentence in county jail or state prison.

Sometimes It's Legal to Possess Marijuana!

IN some states, California being one of them, there is one clearly defined situation in which it is actually legal to possess marijuana. Specifically, in California, it is not unlawful to possess marijuana if it is possessed "solely for the purpose of abandonment, disposal, or destruction," *and* the marijuana was received for the purpose of terminating the unlawful possession of it by another person or preventing another person from acquiring possession of it.

Clearly, the above situation seldom forms the basis of a legal defense to marijuana possession The law was enacted to immunize parents who confiscate marijuana from their kids, as well as to immunize anti-marijuana crusaders who take another person's marijuana and are arrested before they have had an opportunity to destroy the confiscated marijuana or turn it over to the police.

Sale of Marijuana

UNDER the laws of every state, it is a crime to knowingly possess marijuana with the intent to sell or distribute it. This crime is often referred to as "possession for sale." However, it is important to note that many states follow the federal scheme and don't require an actual sale or even an intent to sell. In these states, as under federal law, the prosecution must prove an intent to *distribute* marijuana and not necessarily an intent to sell it.

In order to convict a person possessing marijuana for sale, the prosecution in most states must prove two things: (1) actual or constructive possession, and (2) intent to sell or distribute. Note that unlike the crime of possession, many states do not require the prosecutor to prove that the person possessed a usable amount of marijuana.

The first element (actual or constructive possession) is the same as that discussed in the previous section regarding the crime of possession. The only new element is intent to sell or distribute. Prosecutors often prove the intent element by showing an actual sale. In the alternative, if the police weren't able to catch a suspect in an actual sale, they will attempt to prove the person's intent with circumstantial evidence. For example, by showing that when the police arrested the person they also seized such items as scales, cash, pay-owe sheets, or baggies filled with small accurately weighed quantities of marijuana.

The United States Supreme Court has held that possession of a large amount of a controlled substance may, in and of itself, establish the element of intent to sell or distribute. The case concerned heroin rather than marijuana, so as of now it is unclear what quantity of marijuana the Supreme Court considers large enough to raise the inference of intent to sell.

State courts are all over the board as to how much marijuana must be possessed to circumstantially indicate a person's intent to sell or distribute. In fact, some states are now rewriting their marijuana laws to add new sections that make it a serious crime to possess marijuana "in a sufficient quantity to make it reasonable to believe under all the circumstances, that the marijuana was possessed with the intent to distribute it." In one case a court found that possession of 70 marijuana plants reasonably indicated an intent to distribute. In another case a court found that a defendant's possession of a one-pound brick of marijuana was *insufficient* to uphold the defendant's conviction for possession with intent to distribute.

The case of Roger Davis, decided by a Virginia court, is representative of how many marijuana-sales cases are proven. In this case, Roger was at home when he heard a fateful knock at his front door. The next moment, police officers with a search warrant were in his home. The officers immediately searched Roger. Inside his jacket pocket, they found $800 cash but no marijuana. Feeling scared and intimidated, Roger told the officers that all the marijuana was downstairs in the basement. The officers searched the basement and found a white plastic bag containing a little over 6 ounces of marijuana. They also found a stem from a Cannabis plant, scissors, numerous Cannabis seeds, two boxes of sandwich baggies, and a box of twist ties. One of the boxes was found on top of a scale. Near the scale, were some gram weights and a conversion chart from grams to ounces.

At Roger's trial, a police officer with extensive training and experience in marijuana crimes testified that marijuana is often sold in plastic sandwich baggies secured by twist ties. In addition, the officer testified that the typical marijuana cigarette contains approximately .4 grams of marijuana and that most people who smoke marijuana, but don't sell it, ordinarily keep less than an ounce of the drug on hand. Therefore, the officer testified, an amount of 6 ounces is clearly not consistent with personal use and could only indicate that Roger intended to sell some of the marijuana.

The court held that all this evidence, although circumstantial, was sufficient to support Roger's conviction for possession with intent to distribute marijuana.

Punishment for Possessing Marijuana with the Intent to Sell or Distribute

In every state, and under federal law, possession of marijuana with the intent to sell or distribute is a separate and more serious crime than simply possessing marijuana. In California, the penalty for selling any amount of marijuana is imprisonment for an unspecified duration—usually no more than three years. However, if you were selling to, or employing, a minor (someone under 18 in California) then the punishment is severely increased to between three and nine years in state prison. The penalties are further increased if a sale occurred on school property or in a public park.

Three Odd-Ball Marijuana Crimes

In most states, there are three marijuana crimes similar to selling marijuana. First, in many states, simply *offering* to sell marijuana is a crime. Here, the prosecutor need *not* prove that the person ever possessed marijuana. The prosecutor need only prove that the person offered to sell some marijuana. In California, you can be fined $100 if convicted of offering to sell marijuana.

Second, it is a crime to give marijuana away for free. In California, a person convicted of giving away an ounce or less of marijuana is usually fined $100. However, if the person gave the marijuana to a minor on school property or in a public park, the person could actually go to state prison. Lastly, in many states like California, offering to sell, or actually selling a substance claimed to be marijuana but which is actually a legal substance, is punishable by one year in jail or prison.

Cultivating, Drying, or Processing Marijuana

IN most states, in order to convict for cultivating, drying, or processing marijuana, the prosecution must prove that the person: (1) knew plants were growing on his property, and (2) knew the plants were Cannabis. A person cannot be punished for both cultivation and possession of the same plants. The prosecution must elect one sentence or the other.

In every state, if a person is convicted of cultivating, drying, or processing marijuana, he or she can be sent to prison. Such a conviction goes on the person's record as a felony.

Transportation of Marijuana

IN every state it is a crime to transport *any* amount of marijuana in a vehicle. In California, if you are convicted of transporting 28.5 grams or less, then the fine is $100. However, if you are convicted of transporting more than 28.5 grams, you can be imprisoned for up to four years.

Being in a Room Where Marijuana Is Smoked

IN some states (currently not including California) it is a crime to be in a room where marijuana is being smoked. To convict a person of this crime, the prosecutor usually need only prove that the person: (1) was in the room, and (2) knew that others present were smoking marijuana. The prosecutor does *not* have to prove that the person was also smoking. The punishment for this crime varies from state to state but tends to be similar to the penalty for possessing marijuana.

Driving Under the Influence of Marijuana

IN every state, it is illegal to drive a motor vehicle while under the influence of marijuana. If you are caught driving under the influence of marijuana in California (and you have no prior convictions for driving under the influence of alcohol or a drug), you face a minimum fine of approximately $1,000, two days in county jail, and suspension of your driver's license for up to six months. The details of this crime are discussed in more detail in Chapter 5.

Aiding and Abetting a Marijuana Crime

MOST states have laws that make anyone who knowingly aids in the commission of a crime guilty of that crime. In other words, if you aid in the commission of a crime, you can be convicted and sentenced for the underlying crime itself. Moreover, these laws have been applied in the context of marijuana crimes.

For example, in one case in Washington state, an undercover police officer asked a man if he knew where he could get some marijuana. Not realizing he was talking to an undercover officer, the man replied that his brother had some marijuana and would sell it for $100 an ounce (1981). The officer told the man that $100 was too high, whereupon the man replied that it was "good pot well worth the price." The court held that this statement proved that the man was aiding the sale. Consequently, he was convicted of *selling marijuana*! Many courts have upheld convictions based on a person's arrangement of a meeting between a seller of marijuana and a buyer.

Federal Marijuana Crimes

UNDER the federal government's scheme for regulating and controlling drugs, a drug is placed into one of five "schedules." Those drugs most tightly controlled, and for possession of which the severest penalties may be imposed, are placed in "Schedule I." There are three criteria for placing a drug into Schedule I. The drug must: (1) have a high potential for abuse, (2) have no currently accepted medical use, and (3) lack safety even under medical supervision.

Despite the fact that marijuana has been proven not to be physically addictive, and to be helpful to many people suffering from illness and disease, and has never directly resulted in a single death, the federal government has classified it as a Schedule I drug, along with heroin, morphine, and LSD. Numerous marijuana users have challenged the scheduling of marijuana, arguing that it does not meet the criteria for placement in Schedule I. However, in every case, the courts have rejected these arguments.

The federal laws on marijuana are very similar to the state laws. Therefore, if you are in violation of a state marijuana law, you are very likely also violating a federal marijuana law. As the Supreme Court has interpreted the Double Jeopardy clause of the Fifth Amendment, you can be prosecuted by both the state and the federal governments for a single act. The theory is that the state and federal governments are "separate sovereigns," and your single act can violate the laws of both; hence each sovereign can prosecute you for violating its law. At present, such multiple prosecutions rarely occur, though given the current anti-drug hysteria, the trend may begin moving toward them.

Punishment Under the Federal Law

IF you committed a federal marijuana crime on or after November 1, 1987, and are convicted, the judge will decide your sentence based on the Federal Sentencing Guidelines. These guidelines are contained in Appendix B. In addition, any person convicted of a federal marijuana crime punishable by more than one year in prison is subject to the federal forfeiture laws.

Forfeiture: How You Can Lose Your Cash, Car, or Home

IF you are convicted, or often merely suspected, of engaging in a marijuana crime, the government may try to take any and all property used to "facilitate" your crime. In fact, you may have seen the advertisements for such auctions, at which drug dealer's cars, boats, and homes are auctioned off to the highest bidder. In California alone, more than $130,000,000 worth of assets have been seized under the state forfeiture law since it went into effect in 1989.

Usually the items that the government takes are sold at a public auction and the government keeps the money. In California, approximately 75 percent of the funds go to the state and local law enforcement, another 15 percent to the prosecuting agency. In some states, if the police request it, the property (usually a car) is turned over to the law-enforcement agency that seized it, and is used in undercover operations. Under both federal and state forfeiture laws, any items used to help grow, process, or transport marijuana are subject to forfeiture. In addition, any money furnished "in exchange for a controlled substance" or "traceable to such an exchange" is subject to forfeiture. Likewise, any property purchased with cash derived from marijuana sales can be taken by the government.

As with the various marijuana crimes, the federal government has developed a scheme regulating asset forfeiture as has each of the states. The specifics of each state's forfeiture laws are impossible to detail here. However, as an example, the California state forfeiture laws will be outlined and compared with the federal laws.

Under California's forfeiture laws, forfeiture proceedings can be instituted without any criminal conviction and even without any criminal charges being filed! To make matters even worse, forfeiture proceedings are often considered civil rather than criminal. Under the federal civil forfeiture laws, the legal action by the government is taken against your property, not you. Since you are not the defendant (your property is), your guilt or innocence on the criminal charge is often irrelevant. In other words, even if you are found not guilty in your criminal case, the government can still proceed against your property under the civil forfeiture laws.

Because many forfeiture proceedings are labeled "civil" rather than "criminal," many of the constitutional protections that apply in criminal cases do not apply in forfeiture proceedings. For example, in most states, you have no right to counsel in forfeiture proceedings. (This means the state is not obligated to provide you with counsel if you are unable to afford one. You may, of course, hire your own attorney to represent you at such proceedings, and should do so if your finances allow.) Likewise, both the federal and the state courts are regularly interpreting forfeiture laws in favor of the government. For example, the courts in California have held that an illegal search and seizure (though it will cause the evidence seized to be excluded from *criminal* proceedings) will not immunize the seized property from forfeiture.

In California, forfeiture proceedings move very fast, clearly to the detriment of the "accused." For example, once the prosecution gives notice that it is seeking to seize assets under the forfeiture laws, the defendant must file an answer within only ten days. This is a very short amount of time in which to retain an attorney, especially if the defendant is in custody. The federal scheme gives only a slight reprieve, requiring that the defendant, within twenty days, file a claim stating ownership of the seized property. In either case, failure to file a timely response can result in the property's forfeiture by default.

In California, your car, boat, or plane is subject to forfeiture if it was used to facilitate possession, sale, or growth of five pounds or more of marijuana as measured by the marijuana's dry weight. In addition to the five-pound protection, California has a special exception for cars owned by married people. Under this exception, if one spouse uses the family vehicle to sell more than five pounds of marijuana, and the other spouse is innocent of any wrongdoing, the innocent spouse is permitted to keep the vehicle as long as it is not worth more than $10,000. If the vehicle is worth more than $10,000, the innocent spouse can still keep it, but must pay the state the amount in excess of $10,000.

As noted above, most states can also take any cash, checks, securities, or other things of value that were "furnished or intended to be furnished by any person in exchange for" marijuana. In other words, any money or property that the state can show was obtained by selling marijuana is subject to forfeiture. Moreover, in states like California, the degree of proof that the government must meet is very low. It need only show, by a "preponderance of the evidence," that the property was used to facilitate one of the above-mentioned marijuana crimes. The burden then shifts to you. To keep the property, you must prove your innocence by showing that the property was not used in violation of the drug laws, or that it was so used without your knowledge or consent.

Under federal forfeiture laws, the government must present probable cause that the property is subject to forfeiture. Any property acquired during or shortly after the period of the crime is presumed to be acquired from illegal proceeds from the crime. You may rebut the presumption if you can prove that the property was acquired with legally obtained funds, rather than with "drug money."

In some states, there are a few built-in exceptions that offer some protection against asset forfeiture. For example, in California, as mentioned above, a vehicle is subject to forfeiture only if it was used to facilitate a crime involving five pounds or more of marijuana. In other words, at least under the California law, if a police officer finds a few joints in your car, you are not going to lose your car to the state. The federal law is much harsher. Under the federal scheme, the government can take your vehicle if any marijuana was found inside, or if the vehicle was used in any way to help you commit a marijuana crime. For example, the government took Edna Salas's 1975 Mercedes 280S after a DEA agent found four joints in the ashtray. The agent's affidavit stated:

> I personally searched said vehicle at said location on said date and in the ashtray, located in the area of a vehicle commonly referred to as the "dashboard," I found the partial remains of four (4) cigarette butts, which appeared, in my experience, to be Marihuana. I have been a Special Agent for the Drug Enforcement Administration for approximately eight (8) years (including its predecessor agencies) and I have spent one (1) year as a Criminal Investigator for the United States Bureau of Customs prior to that. I have seen and smelled Marihuana on hundreds of occasions and I am very familiar with its appearance and aroma.

In another case, the federal government took a man's vehicle after finding only "thirteen grains of marijuana" in the vehicle.

The federal "zero tolerance" rule has already been abused by law enforcement. For instance, in July 1992, the police in Oakland, California, feeling too constrained by the state's five-pound rule restricting automobile forfeitures, teamed up with federal DEA agents in a marijuana crackdown. In this sweep, the Oakland police cited 77 marijuana buyers and, using the DEA agent's authority under federal law, confiscated forty-three cars. At least one such seizure occurred after a ten-dollar marijuana deal! In a similar raid two months earlier, thirty-nine cars were seized. Eventually, all but three were returned after the owners paid an "assessment fee."

In addition to taking your cash and your car, the state and federal governments can take your home and real property. Because under the federal law cultivation of marijuana is a felony punishable by more than one year in prison, the federal government can seize your home and real property if even a single Cannabis plant is found on the property. In other words, even if the marijuana was solely for your own personal use and not for sale, it can form the basis for property forfeiture under federal law.

If the federal government finds that you were growing marijuana on your property, it can force you to give up the *entire* piece of property, not just the portion where the marijuana was found growing. For example, in one federal case, a man was charged with possessing more than 700 marijuana plants with intent to distribute them. The evidence was undisputed that all the plants were grown on a very small portion of land. Despite this fact, however, a federal court ordered the forfeiture of the man's *entire 40-acre* parcel of land. In another case, the federal government successfully seized a man's condominium for selling $250 worth of cocaine on the premises.

Many people, after being arrested on a marijuana charge, try to shield their assets from possible forfeiture by transferring title to the property. Suffice it to say that the government is not so easily tricked. To protect against such ploys, the federal government, as well as most states, has created "the doctrine of relation back." Under the relation-back doctrine, the title to property is judged at the time the property was used to commit the crime. Therefore, transferring title in your property after your arrest does no good, since title vests in the government at the time the property was used to commit the crime.

In fact, many absolutely innocent people get caught up in this doctrine when they purchase a vehicle only to learn later, when the government takes it, that it was previously used in a drug deal. These people must then prove their own innocence, by showing that they had no knowledge that the vehicle was ever involved in a drug deal. The attorney fees to handle such a matter often exceed the value of the car; so for practical reasons, many people do not contest the seizure, despite their innocence.

2. Fourth-Amendment Basics

How Big Brother Gets Incriminating Evidence

"The right of the people to be secure in their persons, houses, papers, and effects, against unreasonable searches and seizures, shall not be violated. . . ."
Fourth Amendment to the United States Constitution

Your right to be free from unreasonable governmental searches and seizures is guaranteed by the Fourth Amendment to the United States Constitution. As the Amendment clearly states, all people in the United States are constitutionally protected against unreasonable searches and seizures by government agents.

There is no hard and fast definition of the word "search." However, generally speaking, a search occurs whenever a government agent (such as a police officer) accesses an area in which you have a reasonable expectation of privacy. In the words of the Supreme Court, a "search" occurs when an agent of the government "compromises the individual interest in privacy."

Most courts apply a two-part test to determine whether or not a police officer's action constituted a "search" under the Fourth Amendment. First, the court will examine whether the individual who claims he was "searched" has "exhibited an actual (subjective) expectation of privacy." In other words, the court will look to see what attempts the person made to preserve an area or item as private. Second, the court will examine whether the person's expectation of privacy is "one that society is prepared to recognize as reasonable." In other words, a court will *not* protect a person's expectation of privacy if an average person would find the expectation unreasonable.

A "seizure" occurs when a government agent either takes an item in which you have a possessory interest, or in some way severely restrains your freedom or liberty. Using the words of the Supreme Court, a "seizure" occurs when an agent of the government "deprives the individual of dominion over his or her person or property." In other words, not only can an officer seize your property, but he can also seize you. As will be explained in the next chapter, the law calls an officer's seizure of a person either a "detention" or an "arrest."

The most important question to ask when analyzing the legality of a search or seizure is: "Was it reasonable?" Reread the above clause from the Fourth Amendment, and you'll see that it protects you only against *unreasonable* searches and seizures. Therefore, only those searches that a court determines are *unreasonable* are illegal.

The Exclusionary Rule: The Price the Government Pays for Violating the Fourth Amendment

IF a court decides that a police officer's search or seizure was illegal (i.e., unreasonable), then whatever the officer saw or seized will be excluded from evidence. This is known as the "exclusionary rule," and its purpose is to deter police officers from making illegal searches and seizures. For example, if an officer illegally searches your car and finds 100 pounds of marijuana, the exclusionary rule will prevent the prosecutor from introducing the marijuana in court. Usually this will result in the dismissal of your case for lack of evidence, despite the fact that you were found with 100 pounds of marijuana! (Of course, you don't get the marijuana back!)

It may seem strange to let absolutely guilty people go free, but it turns out that this is the only effective way to force police officers to comply with the Fourth Amendment. In fact, even with the exclusionary rule, police officers are still motivated to conduct illegal searches and seizures because, although the evidence will be excluded from court, the police have obtained the marijuana and forced the person to undergo the stress and embarrassment of being arrested and initially charged with a crime.

One very important aspect of the exclusionary rule is that the rule applies only when a government agent's illegal search or seizure has violated *your* reasonable expectation of privacy. The United States Supreme Court has held that Fourth-Amendment rights are of a personal nature. In other words, even if a police officer has made a clearly illegal search that turned up incriminating evidence against you, you will be unable to assert the exclusionary rule if the officer's search was of another person or another person's property in which you had no reasonable expectation of privacy. Simply put, *you* must have been the victim of the police officer's search in order for the exclusionary rule to apply. For example, police officers in Georgia caught Stephen Karlovich tending a Cannabis garden on some property owned by his friend Thomas. Stephen argued that the officers discovered the Cannabis garden, as well as Stephen's presence there, by way of an illegal search. The court refused to hear Stephen's argument about the illegality of the search after finding that the officers entered Thomas's property, not Stephen's. The court held that, even if the officers' search was illegal, *Stephen* had no constitutional protection because *he* had no reasonable expectation of privacy on Thomas's land.

A counterpart to the exclusionary rule is what's known as the doctrine of the "fruit of the poisonous tree." Under this doctrine, not only is the evidence directly obtained by the illegal search or seizure excluded, but so is any indirect evidence. The fruit-of-the-poisonous-tree doctrine excludes any evidence that the police obtained by "exploiting" an illegal search or seizure. For example, in one case the police illegally searched a man's home and found numerous Cannabis plants. After the search, the police arrested the man and took him to jail. At the jail, the man confessed that he had been growing and selling marijuana for the last three years, ever since losing his job.

The court that heard the man's case held that, because the Cannabis plants were obtained through an illegal search, they must be excluded from evidence. In addition, the court also excluded the man's subsequent confession, because it was obtained after the police made the illegal search and as a result of the illegal search. Because the police obtained the confession by exploiting their earlier illegal search, the man's confession was also excluded from evidence. As a result, although the police found Cannabis plants in the man's home and obtained the man's confession, after the exclusionary rule and the fruit-of-the-poisonous-tree doctrine were applied, no evidence remained. Therefore the man's case was dismissed for lack of evidence.

Do My Rights Depend on Who Searches Me?

Yes! Constitutional rights provide protection only against actions by the *government* (federal or state) or its agents (the most obvious of which are police officers). There is no constitutional protection against unreasonable searches by *private* persons. This rule comes as a great surprise to many people without any legal training, and it is crucial that you understand its effect.

Suppose a private citizen who is an anti-marijuana crusader suspects you of marijuana use. What if that person illegally breaks into your home, steals some of your marijuana, and gives it to the police? There are actual cases of this happening, and the answer is always the same. The marijuana turned over to the police will form the basis for a search warrant for your home. If a police officer's search under that warrant then turns up evidence of marijuana, you will be arrested despite the illegality of your neighbor's action. In addition, neither the exclusionary rule nor the fruit-of-the-poisonous-tree doctrine applies to searches or seizures by private people, and hence the marijuana removed by the thief will be used against you in court. It does not matter that the person obtained the marijuana illegally by breaking into your home. (Of course, you can press criminal charges against your neighbor based on his alleged illegal entry of your home, but that won't help you defend against the marijuana charge against you.)

Note, however, that the rule is different if the police arranged the break-in. In that case, a court would consider the private citizen an agent of the government; so the person's search of your home, and seizure of your marijuana, would be just as illegal as a police officer's. As a result, in such a situation the exclusionary rule would apply, and the marijuana found by the private person as well as the marijuana found during the execution of the search warrant would be excluded from evidence. Simply put, a private citizen who is working for the police *is* subject to the Fourth-Amendment constraints and the exclusionary rule.

The Reoccurring Hotel-Maid Example

BILL was driving from Los Angeles to San Francisco but became tired as he approached Santa Barbara. Upon reaching Santa Barbara, Bill stopped and rented a motel room. Inside his room, Bill rolled a joint and smoked while watching Dragnet. The next morning, Bill woke up and went out to get a bite to eat.

As Bill ate breakfast, he was unaware that a hotel maid was cleaning his room. The maid discovered Bill's personal stash of pot as well as the partially smoked joint. She rushed to the police with the marijuana, reporting that she found it while cleaning Bill's room. The police quickly obtained a search warrant and, upon searching Bill's room, discovered additional evidence that Bill was transporting marijuana. Bill was subsequently convicted of the crime of transporting marijuana.

Analysis: The maid is not a government agent and hence is not limited by the Fourth Amendment. Therefore, even if she was in Bill's room without his permission, or digging through his belongings without his permission, her testimony on what she found in his room will be admissible in court. In this situation the exclusionary rule is inapplicable. Likewise, the search warrant is clearly valid, despite the fact it was based on the maid's theft of Bill's marijuana.

If Bill had understood the limits on the Fourth Amendment, and had been thinking, he would have removed all evidence of marijuana from his hotel room prior to leaving. Most likely, the safest place for such items would have been in a closed opaque container locked in the trunk of his car.

Private Mail Carriers

BECAUSE the Fourth Amendment does not constrain searches by private people, any packages sent through a private mail carrier, such as Federal Express or U.P.S., are subject to warrantless searches, by the carrier's personnel, for any or no reason at all. In practice, private mail carriers have better things to do than dig through mail looking for drugs; therefore such searches usually occur only when something indicates the package may contain drugs. In such cases, the carrier will usually notify the DEA or local law enforcement.

If the DEA or a local police agency is notified by a private mail carrier that a package has been found that is believed to contain marijuana, the agency will send an agent to examine the package. There are many cases discussing the extent to which the law-enforcement agent can conduct a warrantless search of such a package. The rule that has evolved from these cases is that the law-enforcement agent must limit his warrantless search of the package to that already done by the private carrier. The courts have reasoned that a person has no reasonable expectation of privacy in such a limited search, because the contents viewed by the private carrier are now public. In the Supreme Court's words:

> Once frustration of the original expectation of privacy occurs,
> the Fourth Amendment does not prohibit governmental use of
> the now nonprivate information: This Court has held repeat-
> edly that the Fourth Amendment does not prohibit the obtaining
> of information revealed to a third party and conveyed by him
> to Government authorities, even if the information is revealed
> on the assumption that it will be used only for a limited purpose
> and the confidence placed in a third party will not be betrayed.
> The Fourth Amendment is implicated only if the authorities
> use information with respect to which the expectation of
> privacy has not already been frustrated.

If the law-enforcement agent wants to go further than the search conducted by the private carrier, the agent must obtain a search warrant.

Information: How the Police Get It

UNLIKE just about every other crime, marijuana crimes are consensual and very seldom involve what could be considered a "victim." As a result, the police get very little information about marijuana offenses from alleged victims calling to report a crime. Rather, in most cases, the police must actively seek out information. There are numerous means by which law-enforcement agencies gather information about marijuana growers, sellers, and users.

The Citizen Informer

GENERALLY speaking, one of the best sources for information about marijuana crimes is what's termed the "citizen informer." A "citizen informer" is supposed to be a disinterested person who is acting out of civic duty. In most crimes, they are the victims or witnesses of a crime who report the incident to the police. For example, a person who is robbed will call the police, report the robbery, describe the robber, and generally try to assist the police in catching the bad guy. However, with marijuana crimes, citizen informers are often the "concerned" parents of a child who was sold or given marijuana, or anti-marijuana crusaders who believe that marijuana use is evil or dangerous and that it is their civic duty to report any tips they have to the police. For example, the hotel maid in the last example was a citizen informer. Likewise, there are many cases where the citizen informer was a telephone repairman or a cable-television installer who saw evidence of a marijuana crime while inside a person's home and notified the police.

Because citizen informers are not seeking personal or financial gain from their tip, the Supreme Court has ruled that citizen informants are presumptively credible unless there are circumstances indicating otherwise. This means that if a citizen informant calls the police and reports that she has seen evidence of a marijuana crime, the police may rely on that information without having to make any attempts to confirm it.

The Confidential Informant

IN addition to using information supplied by citizen informants, the police regularly use information supplied by "confidential informants." As mentioned above, because of the covert nature of consensual marijuana offenses, there is usually no victim. However, there are often people who are working together to grow, harvest, transport, and/or sell marijuana. If a police officer can figure out a way to do it, he will try to use one such person to get incriminating information about one or all of the others. In other words, a confidential informant is someone, often part of the criminal underworld, who is seeking personal gain from the information they supply to the police. Confidential informants from the criminal underworld often have information that would be almost impossible for the police to obtain on their own.

Unlike the citizen informant, who acts out of a motive supposedly unrelated to personal gain, the confidential informant most often acts from a strong self-interest. These people are often paid money for their tips, or just as commonly are offered special deals on their own criminal cases in exchange for their information about someone else.

The obvious problem with relying on the information supplied by confidential informants is that they may try to pass blame to another person in order to get a lighter or suspended sentence on their own criminal charges or to make a few dollars. For this reason, the Supreme Court has held that the police must try to verify the information supplied by confidential informants to find out if it is reliable. In other words, information supplied by a confidential informant is *not* presumed reliable. However, if an officer has used a particular informer in the past, and that informer has a record of providing accurate information, then the confidential informant will be presumed reliable just like a citizen informant.

How Ron Turned from Selling Marijuana to Selling Information

In one case in Illinois, the police raided Ron's home, seizing nearly 2,000 pounds of marijuana, and $135,000 cash. As if that wasn't enough, the police also found a notebook that recorded in code (easily broken) all of Ron's past marijuana sales.

Needless to say, it did not look good for Ron, and Ron knew it. In order to keep himself out of state prison, Ron made a deal with the prosecutor. The prosecutor agreed to give Ron probation if Ron would provide him with information regarding an even-larger marijuana trafficker. The prosecution had nothing to lose: if Ron's information was no good, the deal would not be honored. On the other hand, if Ron's information was accurate, then the prosecutor would be a big hero for busting the even larger dealer. (And Ron would never again see his marijuana or his money.)

Ron told the police that he knew of a man named Mike whom he had dealt with on several occasions in the past. In fact, Ron reported that he had been to Mike's home a couple of times to help Mike try to cure a mineral deficiency in some of his Cannabis plants. Ron and Mike felt comfortable confiding in one another, because they were both insiders in the world of large-scale Cannabis growing, and accordingly felt that the other would not squeal.

Although Ron felt bad about informing on Mike, he knew it was the only way he could avoid going to state prison. Given such an incentive, Ron told the police officers what he knew about Mike's Cannabis-growing operation.

The police confirmed that a man named Mike lived at the address given by Ron. They also confirmed that Mike drove a 911 Porsche as Ron had said. Based on Ron's information, and the officers' confirmation of some of the details, the police obtained a search warrant to search Mike's home. Inside, they found more than 4,000 pounds of freshly harvested marijuana. Mike was subsequently convicted and sent to state prison. Ron received probation with a very low sentence in county jail.

Undercover Cops and the Doctrine of "Misplaced Trust"

IN addition to citizen informants and confidential informants, law-enforcement agencies gain information by conducting their own undercover operations. These undercover cops, commonly called "narcs," weasel their way into groups suspected of marijuana use, and attempt to gain information that will later be used in criminal prosecutions.

In order to facilitate the work of undercover cops and confidential informants, the courts have developed what's known as the "doctrine of misplaced trust." Under this doctrine, there is no Fourth-Amendment protection when a person unknowingly invites an undercover cop or informant into his home under the mistaken belief that the cop is really a fellow marijuana user, grower, or trafficker. Or, in the words of the Supreme Court, "it is well settled that when an individual reveals private information to another, he assumes the risk that his confidant will reveal that information to the authorities, and if that occurs the Fourth Amendment does not prohibit the governmental use of that information." In other words, the courts universally conclude that individuals take the risk, in all their dealings, that their trust may be betrayed whenever they voluntarily speak with another person.

For example, in one case, Lewis invited a new friend into his home, not knowing that the person was an undercover federal narcotics agent. Lewis spoke freely with his new friend and even sold him marijuana on two occasions. When Lewis was arrested, he argued that the agent's actions were a violation of his right to privacy, and that he never knowingly consented to the agent's warrantless entry of his home. The United States Supreme Court rejected Lewis's argument. The Court explained that whenever someone invites a guest into his home, he takes the risk that the guest will see whatever is in plain view, and may divulge to the authorities what is seen and talked about. It makes no difference that the guest is really an undercover government agent.

Your Kids May Be Used Against You

RECENTLY, again as part of the hysteria created by the government's "War on Drugs," many elementary schools are beginning to include anti-drug education programs in their curriculum. The most popular program is "Drug Abuse Resistance Education," known more commonly by its acronym, DARE. Currently, the program is in about a quarter of all elementary schools.

The program instructors, who are almost all police officers, instruct students that illegal drugs are very bad and that using them makes you a bad person. In addition to the general vilification of all illegal drugs, the officers ask students if they know anyone who uses drugs. Although the program states that no names are used in class discussions, DARE students have later confided in an officer that their parents or siblings smoke marijuana. For example, in one case in Colorado, a ten-year-old boy called the police to report that his parents smoked marijuana. He identified himself as "a DARE kid."

In another case, Mary, a fifth-grader in Maine, visited the police station following a DARE class, and informed them that she knew two people who smoked marijuana: her parents. The police questioned Mary for nearly an hour, and then used her information to obtain a search warrant for her parents' home. The search uncovered some Cannabis plants growing in her parents' bedroom. As a result, Mary's parents were arrested, and subsequently convicted of growing marijuana. Also as a result, Mary has required extensive psychological counseling for feelings of guilt and betrayal.

Your Mail Orders May Be Used Against You

ANOTHER scary trend in law-enforcement information gathering has been revealed in several court decisions. Evidently, in 1989, the DEA subpœnaed the records of companies that advertised hydroponic growing equipment or marijuana-seed catalogs in *High Times* magazine! Once the DEA obtained this information, they forwarded it to local law-enforcement agencies across the country.

In one case, the DEA informed the Missouri-state highway patrol that Mike had received two shipments of merchandise from Superior Growers

Supply, Inc. The state police officer who was given the information drove by Mike's home and verified his address as the one receiving the two shipments. The officer also noticed that the windows of Mike's home were covered with blankets hung horizontally. The officer contacted the electric company and learned that Mike's home used almost four times more electricity than his neighbors' homes did.

Given this information, the officer prepared an affidavit for a search warrant to search Mike's house for marijuana. The officer's affidavit stated:

> Superior Growers Supply, Inc., is a company who sells indoor hydrophonic [sic] growing equipment and grow lights. They advertise in *High Times* magazine, a magazine that specializes in marijuana-growing products and technology, and promotes growing of marijuana and concealment from law enforcement as well as the legalization of marijuana.

> As a law-enforcement officer trained in indoor marijuana-growing operations, I know that indoor-growing operations use large amounts of electricity to operate indoor grow lights and hydrophonic [sic] grow equipment. I also know that blankets are often used to conceal grow lights that are operated 24 hours a day and to obstruct the view of outsiders. The information obtained from the Drug Enforcement Administration identifying individuals who have placed orders with companies such as Superior Growers Supply, Inc. has resulted in indoor-growing operations being located in eight of eight cases that I am aware of.

Given the above information, derived originally from the subpœnaed records of *High Times* advertisers, a judge issued a search warrant for Mike's home. The search uncovered an indoor-growing operation, and Mike was arrested and convicted.

Your Garbage May Be Used Against You

IF you stop to think about it, the various items you discard into your garbage are really a detailed record of your life. Your garbage contains evidence of your most private activities, including what you ate, what you've purchased, where you shop, whether you had sex, and of course, whether you grew or even smoked marijuana. You might think that given the clearly personal nature of garbage, the

Supreme Court would have decided that a search warrant is required for government agents to search your garbage. However, the sad truth is that the Court has decided just the opposite. In a relatively recent case, the Court held that any garbage that a person places on the curb for pickup by his garbage collector can be seized and searched by the police without a warrant! In fact, the police do not even have to have a reasonable suspicion that you're involved in criminal activity before they seize your curb-side garbage. Rather, under the Supreme Court's opinion, a law-enforcement agent can snoop through your curb-side garbage for any reason whatsoever.

In the case that the Supreme Court used to create this rule, a police officer received a tip from a criminal informer that Billy was trafficking in marijuana and other drugs. The officer investigating the tip drove by Billy's house, and observed his garbage on the curb in front of his house, ready for pickup. The officer suspected that Billy's garbage might contain evidence that would verify the informer's information. However, not wanting to tip off Billy by digging through the garbage himself, the officer contacted Billy's garbage collector, and requested that Billy's garbage be kept separate from the other garbage and turned over to the police. The garbage collector followed the officer's order, and upon receiving Billy's garbage bags, the officer searched through them without first obtaining a search warrant.

By sorting through Billy's garbage, the officer found evidence that Billy was using drugs. This information was used to obtain a search warrant for Billy's home. When the police executed the search warrant, they discovered some hashish in Billy's home.

At the trial, Billy's attorney argued that the officer's initial warrantless search of Billy's garbage was unlawful under the United States Constitution. The attorney argued that Billy had placed his garbage in a non-see-through bag, and that he therefore had a reasonable expectation that the contents would remain private. Therefore, his attorney argued, the Fourth Amendment protected Billy's garbage from a governmental search and seizure unless the police first obtained a search warrant.

The Supreme Court disagreed. The Court explained that when Billy placed his garbage bags on the public curb for the garbage collector to take, he had no reasonable expectation that the contents would remain private. Why not? Well, the Court reasoned that common experience indicates that plastic bags filled with garbage and left on the street for pickup are often torn open by dogs and their contents thereby disclosed to everyone. Likewise, such garbage is often snooped through by children and scavengers. In addition, the Court noted that Billy placed his garbage on the curb for the very purpose of turning it over to a third person. For these reasons, the Court concluded that a person has no reasonable expectation of privacy for his or her garbage once it is placed in bags on the curb for pickup by the garbage collector. Therefore, the Court concluded, the warrantless seizure and search of Billy's garbage was legal.

Fortunately, several *state* supreme courts have held that, although the federal constitution may not protect garbage once it is placed on the curb for pickup, the constitution of their state does. Specifically, the Supreme Courts of New Jersey and of Washington have interpreted their own state constitutions as giving greater protection than does the federal constitution. Therefore, in those states, the courts will hold that you retain a reasonable expectation of privacy for your garbage despite the fact that it is placed on the curb for pickup. Accordingly, in New Jersey and Washington, police officers must obtain a search warrant before searching garbage.

Note, however, that because the protection in these states stems from the state constitution, a police officer's warrantless search of your garbage will be excluded only if you are prosecuted in *state* court. If the federal government chooses to prosecute, it is the *federal* constitution that will control the case rather than the state constitution. In that situation, even the state police officer's warrantless search of your garbage would be deemed legal as in Billy's case above, and the evidence used against you in the *federal* prosecution.

3. Encounters with Police

What They Can Do, What You Should Do

The Three Basic Categories of Police-Citizen Encounters

The United States Supreme Court, as well as all the state courts, have held that the reasonableness and hence the legality of a police officer's actions must be judged by examining the circumstances surrounding the action. Generally speaking, all encounters with police officers can be placed in one of three categories: (1) contact, (2) detention, or (3) arrest. Your legal rights during an encounter with a police officer will depend on how the encounter is categorized by a court.

Contact

THE first level of many encounters with police is known as a "contact." A contact occurs when a police officer attempts to engage you in conversation. For example, if an officer asks you for directions, or asks you if you saw something or someone, he is merely "contacting" you. The essential characteristic of a contact is that you remain free to leave at all times. Because you are always free to leave, a contact is not considered a seizure. Since it is not a seizure, and obviously is not a search, the Fourth Amendment does not apply; therefore a police officer is free to contact a person for *any* reason. He does not need even a reasonable suspicion that the person is engaged in criminal activity.

During a contact with a police officer, you are free to behave as you would with any ordinary citizen. You need not identify yourself. You may answer the officer's questions or ignore him and walk away. The United States Supreme Court has made this very clear, stating:

> Law-enforcement officers do not violate the Fourth Amendment by merely approaching an individual on the street or in some other public place, by asking him if he is willing to answer some questions, by putting questions to him if the person is willing to listen, or by offering as evidence in a criminal prosecution his voluntary answers to such questions. . . . The person approached, however, need not answer any question put to him; indeed, he may decline to listen to the questions at all and may go on his way. . . . He may not be detained even momentarily without reasonable, objective grounds for doing so; and his refusal to listen or answer does not, without more, furnish those grounds.

Often an officer will have a hunch that a person is up to something, and hope that by talking to the person he might detect some concrete evidence of a crime, such as possession of marijuana. This commonly occurs in airports when drug-enforcement agents think a person may be transporting drugs, but have no real evidence. In such situations, the agents will often contact the person and inform him that they are conducting a narcotics investigation and would like to talk to him. In such a pressure-packed situation, many people (often those who actually *are* carrying drugs) foolishly agree to speak with the agents, perhaps believing that it would be more suspicious to decline to speak. These conversations often give the agent additional evidence that the person is in possession of drugs, and the person is arrested. In addition, if the person is prosecuted, any statements he made during the contact will be used against him.

Therefore, generally speaking, if you use drugs you should be on your guard whenever you are approached by a police officer who merely engages you in small talk. If you are in possession of marijuana, it is usually best to tell the officer that you are late for an appointment and continue on your way. As will be explained in the next section, unless the officer has a specific reason to believe you are involved in criminal activity, he must respect your wishes and allow you to leave.

Detention

THE second level of citizen-police encounters is referred to as a "detention." A detention occurs whenever an officer's actions or words lead you to reasonably believe that you are *not* free to simply walk away. For example, any time an officer stops a vehicle, orders a person to stop, or orders a person to sit down, the officer's action constitutes a detention of the person.

Unlike a contact, a detention *is* a seizure; so the Fourth Amendment is applicable, and the officer is limited as to when he can detain a person. The courts have universally held that, with a few clear exceptions, an officer can detain a person only if he has a "reasonable suspicion" that the person is involved in criminal activity.

The legal definition of "reasonable suspicion" is ever-changing. The United States Supreme Court has defined reasonable suspicion as requiring "specific and articulable facts which, taken together with rational inferences from those facts, reasonably warrant an intrusion." The important thing to understand is that the reasonable-suspicion standard is *lower* than what's termed "probable cause." In other words, it is quite possible that a police officer will have reasonable suspicion (sufficient to detain a person), but still not have probable cause to believe a person is engaging in criminal activity (needed to arrest the person). In fact, the officer's sole purpose in detaining a person is usually to try to get enough additional evidence to establish probable cause to arrest the person.

Reasonable suspicion exists if an officer can point to some *specific facts* that, taken together, made it reasonable for him, with all his training and experience, to suspect that the person he detained was involved in some illegal activity. In other words, an officer's mere "hunch" is *not* sufficient to detain a person. Rather, the officer must be able to articulate the reasons underlying his suspicion, and the court must agree that his suspicion was reasonable.

The Supreme Court has explained that the purpose of a detention must be limited to the officer's conducting an investigation to find out if there is probable cause to arrest the person detained. Therefore an officer is allowed to detain a person only for the length of time reasonably needed to confirm or dispel his suspicion. If a court finds that an officer detained a person for an unduly long period of time, the court will apply the exclusionary rule to any evidence that the officer found after he exceeded the reasonable time needed to conduct his investigation.

In almost all cases, it is a *series* of facts which, *viewed in combination*, add up to a reasonable suspicion that a person is engaged in criminal conduct. For example, in almost every state, smoking a hand-rolled cigarette is *not*, by itself, sufficient reason for an officer's detention of the smoker. However, when the officer states that he also smelled the odor of burning marijuana, or that the suspect acted extremely nervous at the officer's approach, the totality of the factors may give rise to a reasonable suspicion of criminal activity (and maybe even probable cause sufficient to arrest), thereby allowing the officer to detain the person. Similarly, most courts hold that the fact that a person runs when he sees the police is *not*, by itself, grounds to detain that person. However, when evasive conduct is coupled with other factors such as a "high-crime area" or an officer's observation of other suspicious actions, many courts will permit the officer to detain the person. Note, however, that if flight occurs *after* an officer has formed a reasonable suspicion to detain a person and has ordered the person to stop, the attempt to escape automatically transforms the reasonable suspicion into probable cause, and hence the officer can arrest the person.

Detaining Your Belongings

NOT only can police detain *you* if they have a reasonable suspicion you are violating a marijuana law, they can also detain your belongings if they have a reasonable suspicion that they contain marijuana. Again, a common example occurs in airports when police detain a person because they believe that his luggage may contain marijuana. In such a situation, the police can detain the luggage only for the reasonable time necessary to conduct their investigation. They cannot open the luggage without a search warrant or without the person's consent; therefore they must usually either quickly obtain a search warrant or release the luggage back to the person. Often in such a situation they will have a marijuana-detecting dog sniff the luggage, and will return it if no drug is detected. If marijuana is detected, then they will either arrest the person immediately or quickly obtain a search warrant to open the luggage.

Demanding to See Your Identification

IF an officer legally detains you, most courts now permit the officer to demand to see proof of your identification. In such situations, it's usually best to politely provide the officer with your ID. Nothing is gained by attempting to conceal your identification once you have been legally detained. Similarly, it is not prudent to give a police officer a fake name once you have been lawfully detained or arrested. When a false name is given, the police almost always quickly discover that the person is lying and you can then be charged with the additional crime of giving false information to a police officer. Furthermore, your evasiveness can later be used against you to show your consciousness of guilt and thereby to prove that you knew you possessed marijuana or some other illegal drug. (See Chapter 1 on the "knowledge" element that must be proven to convict a person of possessing marijuana.)

Frisks or Pat-Searches

If a police officer contacts or legally detains a person, the officer may have a right to "frisk" or "pat-search" the person. A frisk is intended only to protect the officer or the public; so an officer can conduct a frisk or pat-search anytime he reasonably fears for his safety or the safety of others.

A frisk is therefore a *limited search* for the sole purpose of detecting a concealed weapon. When conducting a frisk, an officer can pat or feel only the *outside* of a person's clothing. The officer can reach inside a pocket only if he detects a hard object that he reasonably believes could be used as a weapon. The courts of every state have held that almost any hard object justifies the officer in reaching inside the person's pocket to find out if the object is really a weapon.

Courts will uphold a police officer's frisk whenever the officer can state specific facts that lead him to reasonably believe the person was a threat and might possess a weapon. The Supreme Court has instructed that courts should find an officer's frisk illegal if the officer was really looking for drugs rather than weapons. Similarly, courts should find a frisk illegal if an officer went beyond the permissible scope of a frisk and removed *soft* objects or searched *inside* pockets without first detecting a hard object.

It is important to understand that if an officer, while conducting a frisk, feels a hard object that he believes to be a weapon, can remove that object. If he happens to also feel something else in that pocket (such as a joint or baggie of marijuana), he can "accidentally" also pull that out. In fact, such "mistakes" are quite common, and the resulting incriminating evidence is often admissible.

For example, in one case, Officer Carrillo of the Los Angeles Police Department stopped Larry Atmore because Larry allegedly met a description of a murder suspect. When Officer Carrillo pat-searched Larry, he felt a round cylindrical object in Larry's jacket pocket. The officer had information that the murder suspect used a shotgun in the murder, and suspected that the cylindrical object was a shotgun shell.

For that reason, the officer reached into Larry's jacket pocket and removed the object , which, in fact, turned out to be a lipstick case. However, as Officer Carrillo removed the lipstick case, he also removed a joint. Although

Larry was cleared as the murder suspect, he was subsequently convicted of possessing marijuana.

The court held that Officer Carrillo's removal of the joint was legal, because it occurred innocently and in conjunction with his removal of what he believed was a shotgun shell. The court stated, "There is no compelling evidence that Officer Carrillo consciously seized the cigarette. A legitimate implication from the record is that his hand emerged with more than he intended to remove from the pocket. We have all done the same thing when fumbling for keys or coins. There is nothing sinister about it. Once the cigarette was in plain sight, the officer did not have to ignore it."

As an aside, it is interesting to note that the court found the shotgun shell, without a shotgun, to be a "weapon." Why? Well, the court "reasoned" that if the object had been a shotgun shell as Officer Carrillo believed, the shell could have been detonated by any object, and given that Larry was suspected of murder at the time the officer pat-searched him, "The officer could reasonably believe that any sharp object could be used as a detonator. He had not eliminated the possibility that [Larry] might be the person who was sought for murder and who, if caught, could face the death penalty. If he was the murder suspect, he might want to explode the shell even in a way that might entail considerable personal risk to himself, so long as he might escape in the ensuing confusion." Clearly, the lesson to be learned from Mr. Atmore's misfortune is that it is not prudent to carry marijuana in the same pocket with a weapon or even a hard container.

Additionally, it sometimes happens that an officer who legally conducts a pat-search for weapons feels an object which, based on his experience and training, he believes to be marijuana or some other illegal drug. For example, in one case, Lee was legally stopped by an officer who suspected that he might be carrying a concealed weapon. As the officer pat-searched Lee, he felt a *soft* object that made a rustling and crumpling sound when pressed. Although the officer knew it was not a weapon, he suspected it was a baggie of marijuana. The officer reached into Lee's pocket and removed a baggie containing "green vegetable matter." The lab test later confirmed that the substance was marijuana, and Lee was charged with possession.

Lee argued to the court that the officer's removal of the baggie was illegal because the officer knew it was not a weapon before he reached into Lee's pocket. Therefore, Lee argued, the officer had exceeded the permissible scope of a legal pat-search for weapons. Consequently, the marijuana was illegally removed from his pocket and should therefore be excluded from evidence.

At the hearing on this issue, the officer testified that he was a 19-year veteran of the police force, and had received approximately 40 hours of education on identifying drugs, including marijuana. The officer stated that during his 19 years, he had arrested more than 500 people possessing marijuana. The officer concluded that given all his training and experience, he was able to deduce, just by feeling the outside of Lee's pocket, that inside was a baggie of marijuana.

Based on such testimony, the prosecutor argued that the officer's pat-search, while conducted for weapons, unexpectedly turned up probable cause that Lee was in possession of marijuana. This probable cause permitted the officer to reach inside Lee's pocket and seize the marijuana even though he knew it was not a weapon. The court agreed with the prosecutor's argument. Therefore the officer's search of Lee's pocket was deemed legal on the basis that the pat-search developed probable cause of marijuana possession.

The United States Supreme Court has been constantly expanding the permissible scope of an officer's search for weapons after detaining a suspect. At present, the Court permits police officers not only to pat-search the outside of a suspect's clothing, but also to search the immediate area surrounding the suspect. As will be explained in Chapter 5, an officer who legally stops a person's vehicle, and reasonably believes that an occupant is dangerous, can search the car's passenger compartment for weapons.

The Exception to the Reasonable-Suspicion Rule

As explained earlier, an officer's detention of a person is usually legal only if the officer had a reasonable suspicion that the person was involved in criminal activity. However, as with just about every legal rule, there are a few exceptions. If any of these exceptions applies, the officer can automatically (without reasonable suspicion) detain a person.

You may be automatically subjected to detention by a police officer if you fall into any of the following categories:

1. you fit a "drug-courier profile,"
2. you are stopped at a roadblock (discussed in Chapter 5),
3. you are crossing a border or are subject to a border inspection (discussed in Chapter 4), or
4. you look young, and an officer reasonably believes you are a juvenile who is skipping school or violating a curfew.

The Drug-Courier Profile (The First Exception to the Reasonable-Suspicion Rule)

THE Drug Enforcement Administration has developed what is referred to as the "drug-courier profile." The profile was derived from statistical information gained from numerous arrests of persons attempting to transport illegal drugs. Although it is very careful about how it phrases this rule, the United States Supreme Court and almost every state court have held the fact that a person fits the DEA's drug-courier profile is, by itself, reasonable suspicion of criminal activity sufficient for an officer to legally detain the person. In other words, if your appearance and behavior fits the drug-courier profile, you are giving an officer a free shot at legally detaining you.

Obviously, it is important for a person who wants full protection against detentions by law-enforcement personnel to keep himself outside of the profile. However, as you might expect, the DEA has attempted to keep secret the characteristics that make up the profile. Fortunately, numerous cases have been litigated, and from the resulting court opinions one can deduce just what it is that the agents look for.

It turns out that there are seven primary characteristics to the drug-carrier profile, and four secondary characteristics. The seven primary characteristics are:

1. arrival from or departure to an identifiable source city for drugs,
2. carrying little or no luggage, or carrying several empty suitcases,
3. having an unusual itinerary, such as a rapid turnaround time after a lengthy airplane trip,
4. use of an alias,
5. carrying unusually large amounts of currency (thousands of dollars),
6. purchasing airline tickets with a large amount of small denomination currency, and
7. unusual nervousness beyond that ordinarily exhibited by passengers.

The four secondary characteristics to the drug-carrier profile are:

1. using public transportation, particularly taxicabs, in departing from the airport;
2. immediately making a telephone call after deplaning,
3. leaving a false call-back telephone number with the airline, and
4. excessively frequent travel to drug source and distribution cities.

To make matters even more complicated, the profile changes depending on the airport or the area of the country. The specific profiles for the following airport/locations are derived from court opinions.

La Guardia Airport, New York City

1. carrying little baggage,
2. nervousness,
3. checking to see if being followed,
4. attempting to leave the airport immediately,
5. unusual dress,
6. no tags on luggage,
7. attempts by individuals to conceal that they're traveling together.

New Orleans

1. nervousness,
2. little or no luggage
3. large amounts of cash in small bills,
4. unusual itinerary,
5. arriving from drug-source city,
6. paying for ticket in small bills,
7. buying only a one-way ticket,
8. using an alias,
9. using a false telephone number on flight reservation,
10. placing a call immediately on arrival.

Detroit Airport

1. buying ticket with small bills,
2. travel to or from drug-source cities in short time period,
3. empty suitcases or luggage,
4. nervousness,
5. use of alias.

Cleveland Airport

1. purchase of round-trip ticket to and from drug-distribution city, with short stay between flights,
2. purchase of tickets with cash,
3. checking no luggage or empty bags,
4. use of alias,
5. suspicious or nervous behavior.

As you can tell from the above descriptions, the drug-courier profiles are usually restricted to justifying detentions at or near airports. However, in one recent case, a drug-courier type of profile was used to justify the stop of a vehicle, and the subsequent arrest of its driver, for transporting marijuana. In this case, DEA agents were driving an unmarked car on the coast of North Carolina in an area that they believed was used for drug trafficking. While on patrol, the agents observed two vehicles that appeared to be traveling together. They followed the vehicles for about twenty miles, during which time they observed that one of the vehicles was a pickup truck with a camper shell. In addition, the agents noticed that the truck appeared to be heavily weighed down. Lastly, the windows of the truck's camper shell were covered with some type of woven material—not curtains. Based on these observations, the agents suspected that the truck was transporting marijuana. They stopped the truck and, upon searching it, found a large quantity of marijuana.

The United States Supreme Court examined the legality of the agent's stop of the truck and concluded that the stop was constitutional. The court reasoned that the factors relied on by the agents all combined to justify the agents' belief that the vehicle was carrying contraband. The Court emphasized that experienced DEA agents have learned that pickup trucks with camper shells are often used to transport large quantities of marijuana. Additionally, the truck appeared heavily laden, and its windows were covered with some material other than curtains. Accordingly, the vehicle matched the profile of one which is likely to be carrying marijuana, and hence the agents were justified in stopping it to investigate the nature of its cargo.

Juvenile Truants and Curfew Violators (The Fourth Exception to the Reasonable-Suspicion Rule)

In many states, as in California, if an officer reasonably believes that a truancy violation is occurring, he may legally detain the suspected youth and require him to identify himself. If the officer learns that the youth is indeed skipping school, he may return the youth to school or to his or her parents or guardian. The officer may not transport the juvenile to the police station or question him or her about unsolved crimes. Similarly, if a local government has established a curfew for juveniles, most states allow an officer who suspects a possible violation to detain the person and require proof of the person's age. The courts of most states have held that an adult's "youthful appearance" *is* sufficient for an officer to detain that person if prior to the detention the officer reasonably believes the person to be a juvenile who is violating a curfew or skipping school. However, once such a person shows proof that he or she is not subject to the curfew, the officer must immediately permit the person to continue on his way.

Arrest

THE third and final level of citizen-police encounters is the arrest. An arrest occurs when a police officer severely restrains a person's freedom, tells the person that he or she is under arrest, or takes the person into custody. Chapter 6 will discuss in detail what to do if you are arrested on a marijuana charge. For now, you need know only that, in order to arrest a person in public, an officer must have *probable cause* to believe that the person committed a crime. Probable cause to arrest a person exists where the facts and circumstances would lead a reasonable person to believe that the person was guilty of the crime for which he was arrested. Or, in the words of the United States Supreme Court, "probable cause exists where the facts and circumstances within [the police officers'] knowledge and of which they had reasonably trustworthy information [are] sufficient in themselves to warrant a man of reasonable caution in the belief that an offense has been or is being committed." As you can see, an officer's mere suspicion that you are breaking the law, even if reasonable, is insufficient to arrest you.

For now, you should simply understand that probable cause is a higher standard than the reasonable-suspicion standard required for a detention. In other words, any time a police officer has probable cause, he also has, by definition, reasonable suspicion. As will be explained later, an officer can conduct a full-blown search (not just a pat-search) of any person he arrests.

Richard and an Escalating Encounter

RICHARD was at the library one evening looking for a good book. As he thumbed through a book, Officer Friday, in full uniform, walked up next to him, and began looking at another book. Feeling nervous because of Friday's close vicinity, Richard took the book he was looking at and began to leave the aisle. As Richard walked down the aisle away from Friday, the officer said, "Excuse me, is that *The Home Gardener's Guide* you have there?"

Richard responded, "No," and continued walking away from Officer Friday.

Officer Friday scurried around the bookshelf and blocked Richard's path. Officer Friday told Richard that he matched the description of a robbery suspect, and ordered Richard to provide identification. Officer Friday then escorted Richard to his patrol car, and awaited the robbery victim's arrival to positively identify Richard as the robber.

The victim arrived in about five minutes, and stated that Richard was not the person who robbed him. The victim also told Friday, "I told you that the guy who robbed me was about six feet tall and weighed between 300 and 400 pounds. This guy (referring to Richard) is much shorter and only weighs about a hundred pounds! He obviously isn't the guy who robbed me." Officer Friday sheepishly allowed Richard to leave and apologized to the victim for his mistake.

In this example, Officer Friday's first action of approaching Richard and asking about the book is properly classified as a "contact." Richard was free to leave at that point and began to do so. However, most courts would hold that the contact quickly escalated into a "detention" when Officer Friday blocked Richard's path and ordered him to produce identification. Every court would agree that a detention occurred when officer Friday ordered Richard to wait by his patrol car until the burglary victim arrived.

Likewise, every court would hold that the detention was unconstitutional because, based on the victim's description of the robbery suspect, the officer was unreasonable in suspecting that Richard could have been the burglar. Therefore, had the officer pat-searched Richard and subsequently discovered some marijuana, it would have been excluded from court, because it was the product of an illegal detention by Officer Friday.

4. Search Warrants
&
Searches without a
Warrant

Search Warrants: Reasonable and Unreasonable Searches

As was briefly explained in the introduction to Chapter 2, only *unreasonable* searches by police officers are illegal and result in the exclusion of evidence found during such a search. Therefore officers, who know the law, will always try to make their search of a person or place appear reasonable. The best way for a police officer to guarantee that his search is reasonable is for him to obtain a search warrant authorizing the search. However, obtaining a search warrant takes time, as well as additional effort; so police officers seldom go to the trouble to obtain one. Instead, most officers have many other ways to make their warrantless searches appear reasonable to the judge who will eventually decide whether the search was legal.

As a general rule, searches conducted without a warrant are automatically *unreasonable* and hence violate the Fourth Amendment. This means that a court is predisposed to exclude from evidence anything that was found during a warrantless search. However, because courts hate the exclusionary rule, they have developed several exceptions to the warrant requirement that can make a warrantless search reasonable and therefore legal. If a police officer can justify his warrantless search under one of these exceptions, then his search will be deemed legal, and the exclusionary rule will not apply. This chapter will examine the warrant exceptions and attempt to inform you when a police officer can legally search without a warrant.

When dealing with warrantless searches, a crucial concept is whether the person searched had a "reasonable expectation of privacy" in the area searched. For example, homes and offices are considered very private and hence are highly protected against warrantless searches. In contrast, automobiles, trash cans, and public places are considered less private and hence receive less, and in some cases no, protection. Accordingly, a warrantless search of a home may be illegal, whereas the same warrantless search of a car is legal. This idea of a reasonable expectation of privacy underlies all the warrant exceptions.

The Exceptions to the Warrant Requirement (When a Cop's Search and Seizure Is Legal Even Though He Doesn't Have a Warrant)

As a general rule, a police officer can legally conduct a warrantless search or seizure if it falls within one or more of the following categories:

1. The search was conducted after a person is lawfully arrested. (See Chapter 8.)

2. The search was of an automobile, and the officer had probable cause to believe that the vehicle contained contraband. (See Chapter 5.)

3. The person voluntarily consented to the search.

4. The item seized was in plain view of the officer, and its illegal nature was immediately apparent.

5. The search was conducted at a United States border.

6. An immediate search was necessary to preserve evidence.

7. The person or property searched is that of a student at a public school, and the search is by a school official.

As was stated earlier, relatively few searches are conducted with a search warrant. In fact, in the last eight years the United States Supreme Court has reviewed 30 drug cases involving a disputed search or seizure. In 28 of those cases, no search warrant was present. As you will see, for the vast majority of searches, police officers attempt to fit their warrantless search into one of the above categories. If the officer is successful, his warrantless search will be deemed reasonable and therefore legal. As noted above, the first two exceptions are discussed in later chapters. The remaining exceptions are discussed as follows.

Consenting to a Search
(Third Exception to the Warrant Requirement)

AMONG the general public, the law concerning consent is perhaps the most misunderstood. The general rule is that if a person consents to a warrantless search, the search automatically becomes reasonable and therefore legal. Consequently, whatever an officer finds during such a search will be used to convict the person. Simply put, if a person consents to a search, he has waived the primary protection offered by the Fourth Amendment.

Police officers are often pretty tricky about trying to get someone to consent to a search. They know that most people feel intimidated by police officers and will do whatever an officer asks them. For example, the average citizen whose vehicle is stopped by a police officer who says, "Would you mind opening the trunk, please?" will probably consent to the officer's search without thinking or knowing that they have every right to deny the officer's request.

It is absolutely astounding how many people get arrested only because they consented to a search by an officer who then found some marijuana on them or in their bag or car. Evidently these poor souls either were too polite to refuse the officer's request to search their belongings or did not understand that they had a constitutional right to refuse to consent. In most cases, without even knowing it, people relinquish a substantial portion of their Fourth-Amendment rights by consenting to an officer's request to search. Remember, the very fact that the Fourth Amendment exists is proof positive that some very intelligent people who founded our country were aware that a *constitutional* right was needed to protect people from out-of-control police officers. You should never let yourself feel guilty about asserting your constitutional rights, particularly when they are all that stand between your freedom and your being arrested on a marijuana charge.

The sad fact is that most people believe that when an officer approaches them and asks permission to search their person or enter their home, that they are required to grant the officer's request. The truth is the exact opposite—you have a right to associate with and speak to whomever you please. In this respect, there is nothing special about a police officer. Assuming you would not let a complete stranger look through your purse or search your pockets, why would you allow a police officer to do so—especially if you knew you were in possession of marijuana?

For example, if Officer Bacon approaches a person and asks, "Do you mind if I look in your backpack?" he is asking the person to consent to a search. His question is no different from asking, "Would you please give up your Fourth-Amendment right and allow me to look in your backpack?" If, *for any reason* you don't want the officer digging through your belongings, you should refuse to consent by saying something like, "Yes, I do mind. I have private, personal items in my backpack and do not want you looking through them."

The point is that whenever a police officer asks your permission to search, you are under no obligation to consent. The only reason he's asking is that he doesn't yet have enough evidence to forcibly search. By consenting you are giving up one of the most important constitutional rights you have.

Generally speaking, a person gains nothing by consenting to a police officer's request to conduct a warrantless search. The many court cases on the subject, reveal the great danger that often accompanies the waiver of the constitutional right to remain free from such searches. Just remember, any officer who asks your permission to search is looking for evidence that he doesn't have—yet. Little is to be gained and much can be lost by waiving a constitutional right.

If an officer hassles you when you refuse to consent to a search, just tell him that you have personal items and you object to his violating your constitutional right to privacy. If the officer still proceeds to search you and find marijuana, your attorney can argue that the marijuana was discovered through an illegal search and hence should be thrown out of court.

How Mr. Puff Properly Asserted His Constitutional Rights

OFFICER Friday stopped Mr. Puff's vehicle because his registration was expired, and asked Mr. Puff, "Would you please empty the contents of your pockets?"

Mr. Puff properly said, "Are you asking me to empty my pockets, or are you ordering me to empty my pockets?" When Friday said he was simply *asking*, Mr. Puff properly said, "No thanks, and I really must be going."

Analysis: Mr. Puff's question to Friday was entirely appropriate. In fact, Mr. Puff's response was an effective method of turning the table on the officer. If Friday had told Mr. Puff that he was ordering him to empty his pockets, Mr. Puff could have properly responded, "Get a search warrant. I do not consent to your search and would like to continue on my way." That way, if the officer had proceeded to search Mr. Puff's pockets without a warrant, Mr. Puff's lawyer could argue that the search was illegal. If Mr. Puff had consented, his lawyer would have no argument.

The Plain-View Rule
(Fourth Exception to the Warrant Requirement)

As was briefly explained earlier, a "search" occurs whenever a government agent accesses an area in which a person has a reasonable expectation of privacy. A clear example of a "search" is an officer's opening of a person's purse and looking inside for marijuana. In such a case, the person whose purse the officer searched clearly had a reasonable expectation of privacy in its contents, and hence the officer's opening of the purse would be considered a "search." The next question would be whether the officer had a warrant to search the purse or whether his search was within one of the exceptions to the warrant requirement. On the other hand, if an officer's conduct is *not* considered a "search," it doesn't even trigger the Fourth Amendment.

For example, suppose the purse in the above example was made of a clear, see-through plastic that allowed the contents of the purse to be seen by all who passed by. In that case, if an officer saw some marijuana in the purse, it would be in plain view, and the officer would immediately have probable cause to search the purse. A court would hold that the officer's observation of the marijuana was *not* a search, since it invaded no reasonable expectations of privacy.

In many cases, the plain-view rule operates in conjunction with the "exigent circumstances rule" discussed later in this chapter. It is important to understand, (and many police officers simply do not understand this) that observation of marijuana that is in plain view gives an officer *only* probable cause to search or seize. In such a case, the officer has several options. First, if he has probable cause that a person is in possession of marijuana and if that person is in a public area, the officer can arrest the person and conduct a full-blown search incident to the arrest.

However, if the marijuana is seen *inside* a home in plain view by an officer who is *outside* the home, the plain-view sighting gives the officer only probable cause to believe that marijuana can be found in the home. The officer still needs either a warrant, exigent circumstances, or consent to enter the home. In contrast, if an officer sees marijuana in plain view inside an automobile, and the officer is outside the automobile, the automobile exception (see Chapter 5) allows the officer to enter the car without a warrant and immediately seize the contraband. The reason for the different rules? A person inside a home is reasonably entitled to more privacy than a person inside a car.

The primary limit on the plain-view rule is that the officer's view must have been legally obtained. In other words, in order for the plain-view rule to come into effect, the officer must have had a legal right to be in the place from which he saw the contraband. For example, if an officer is in your home pursuant to your consent and he happens to see some marijuana on your kitchen table, a court will consider the officer legally entitled to his view of the marijuana and uphold the officer's warrantless seizure of the marijuana.

In contrast, if the officer was *illegally* inside your home when he saw the marijuana, a court would find that although the marijuana was in plain view, the officer was not legally entitled to that view. Therefore his warrantless seizure of the marijuana would be considered illegal, and the exclusionary rule would apply. There will be more examples of the plain-view rule in the chapters to follow.

How Wayne Learned the Hard Way about the Plain-View Rule

OFFICER Bacon stopped Wayne's car because Wayne's brake lights were not working. The officer approached Wayne's car and asked Wayne to step out. Officer Bacon then asked Wayne for his driver's license and vehicle registration. When Wayne opened his wallet to remove his driver's license, Officer Bacon saw a joint in Wayne's wallet. Officer Bacon immediately searched Wayne, as well as the inside of his car. Inside Wayne's glove box, the officer found more than 100 marijuana joints. Wayne was arrested and convicted.

Analysis: Officer Bacon observed the first joint in plain view when Wayne opened his wallet. The fact that Wayne possessed even a single joint gave the officer probable cause to search the rest of Wayne's person as well as the passenger compartment of his car.

The moral of the story is obvious. First, people who smoke pot are less likely to be stopped if they keep their cars in working order. Second, those who use marijuana would be prudent to keep it away from their driver's license, registration, and any other objects or areas into which they might have to reach if stopped by a police officer. You'd be surprised how many people keep their marijuana on top of their sunvisor with their car registration, and never stop to think about the problem that could present if stopped by the police.

Plain-View Paraphernalia

NOT only can a police officer seize marijuana that he observes in plain view, but he can also seize any items that he has probable cause to believe are used for criminal activity. Examples of specific items that many states allow an officer to seize on sight include identifiable items of marijuana paraphernalia, such as pipes and roach clips.

Most states allow an officer to seize a pipe only if something about it indicates it is used to smoke marijuana. Likewise, most state courts have ruled that a roach clip, by itself, is usually not seizable unless it holds the remnants of a joint or is seen accompanied by other indicia of marijuana use.

Distinct Drug-Carrying Devices (Part of the Plain-View Rule)

IF you were to observe someone walking down the street carrying an electric-typewriter case, you would be reasonable to assume that the case is either empty or contains a typewriter. In a similar vein, courts have held that certain containers are "distinct *drug*-carrying devices." If an officer observes such a container, the courts of most states allow the officer to immediately seize and search the container without a warrant.

In most states, the following containers have been held to be distinct drug-carrying devices and can therefore be searched and seized without a warrant: small glassine envelopes, clear baggies filled with leafy substances, paper bindles, small party balloons filled with a powdery substance, and large blocks wrapped with dark garbage bags and taped with duct tape. Clearly, when at all possible, a person should not have in his or her possession such items, nor should marijuana ever be stored or transported in such containers. To do so simply screams out to the police, "I'm in possession of illegal drugs, feel free to search and arrest me!"

In one case, a Florida police officer suspected that Torin Thompson was carrying a weapon inside of a shaving kit. The officer approached Torin and asked him for identification. Torin stated that his identification was inside the shaving case. The officer pat-searched the outside of the case, and after detecting no weapon allowed Torin to reach inside to retrieve his identification. When Torin pulled his billfold from the case, a small, brown manila envelope fell out onto the hood of his car, and Torin quickly but quietly attempted to brush it to the ground. The officer saw the envelope, picked it up, opened it, and inside found marijuana. The Florida court held that the officer's warrantless opening of the manila envelope was illegal, because, although some brown manila envelopes may contain marijuana, "It cannot be said that most brown manila envelopes contain marijuana. There could have been any number of items in the envelope other than marijuana that Torin would wish to keep private." The court also stated that Torin's conduct in attempting to hide the envelope by brushing it to the ground, "was no different than if he had simply told the officer that he did not want him to look into it without a search warrant." Most courts would probably agree with the Florida court that brown manila envelopes are not distinct marijuana-carrying devices.

The Arizona Supreme Court has, in effect, held that brick-shaped, dark plastic garbage bags are distinctive marijuana-carrying devices. In this case, Dennis Million and two of his friends were observed at approximately 11:00 P.M. one evening, "carrying dark-colored garbage bags and packing them in various compartments within a [motor home]." After loading the motor home, the men began driving toward the California border. As they approached the border between Arizona and California, DEA agents stopped the vehicle, conducted a warrantless search, and recovered a total of 1,238 pounds of marijuana.

Dennis argued that the agents' warrantless search of the plastic garbage bags was illegal because those bags were not distinct marijuana-carrying devices. However, the prosecutor defeated this argument by careful questioning that convinced the court that, to an experienced DEA agent, the plastic bags were recognizable as distinct drug-carrying devices:

Q: What type of garbage bag—you have used the word garbage bag— what type of garbage bags were they carrying that you observed at first?

A: They were the dark large type that you would put in an outside garbage can. Dark green or black. They appeared very dark.

Q: Did they appear to be empty or full?

A: No, sir, they appeared to contain various objects in them that were—that they would bend when they would carry them. The garbage bags would bend and loose objects inside them could be observed.

Q: How would you describe these objects you saw in the bags?

A: Well, they were individual objects, not large. I would describe them, as from prior experiences, as brick-shaped objects.

Q: Have you seen these types of garbage bags on prior occasions?

A: Yes, sir.

Q: How many prior occasions?

A: A 100 or 150 times.

Q: Have those been in connection with investigations of marijuana?

A: Yes, sir.

Q: Is there anything unusual, anything common about the garbage bags, put it that way?

A: In this area, it is most common to find garbage bags of this type to contain marijuana contraband. They are available everywhere.

Q: Is there some reason why garbage bags are used instead of cardboard boxes?

A: One thing, they contain the smell better. Second, they are water-proof. They are able to pack them on different configurations very readily by pushing and shoving them into different locations in the compartment. They put talcum on them to deaden the odor.

The rule about distinct drug-carrying devices is a good example of one which, if known, can be used in the public's favor. For example, there are two nice aspects to the courts' defining what containers can be searched on sight. First, the public is put on notice never to hold or transport marijuana in such containers. Second, in deciding some of these cases, the courts have clearly stated that certain items are *not* distinct drug-carrying devices.

For example, in California, film canisters (the little ones with black bodies and black or light-gray caps) are *not* considered distinct drug-carrying devices; so they cannot be searched without a warrant. Other such "safe" containers include opaque pill bottles, cigarette packs, and any other containers commonly used to carry legitimate items.

Abandoning Marijuana: "Dropsy Cases"

IN many marijuana cases, police officers claim that as they approached a suspect they saw him drop a baggie containing "green leafy vegetable matter believed to be marijuana." The officer then reports that he picked up the baggie and found that it did in fact contain marijuana. It is interesting to note that following the Supreme Court's 1961 ruling, holding that the exclusionary rule bars the admission of evidence in state as well as federal courts when the evidence is the product of an illegal search or seizure, there was a significant jump in the number of cases in which police officers claimed that a person dropped drugs as tne officers approached. For example, one study of New York City police officers showed a near 80 percent increase in the number of cases in which people allegedly abandoned drugs. Clearly, the increase could be explained if officers had begun fabricating the alleged abandonments in order to escape the exclusionary rule following what was really an illegal search.

The general rule on these cases (known as "dropsy" cases) is that an officer can retrieve the marijuana based on either the plain-view rule or on a theory that the drugs were abandoned. The officer can then arrest the person for possession because he has probable cause to believe that the person did possess marijuana. For example, Paul was a musician in a band playing at a local bar. In between sets he stepped outside for some fresh air and smoked a joint. As he stood there enjoying his respite, he noticed a car slowly driving toward him. Not particularly worried, he took another drag on his joint and suddenly noticed that the car was in fact a police patrol car. In shock, and without thinking, Paul threw his joint to the ground and stood there looking at the patrol car.

Officer Bacon, inside the patrol car, observed Paul throw down a lit cigarette (littering) and, suspecting he might turn up some other evidence of crime, got out of his car to speak with Paul. As Officer Bacon bent to retrieve the cigarette, he discovered it was actually a marijuana joint. Because the officer had observed Paul toss the joint on the ground, the officer had probable cause to arrest Paul and search him for additional marijuana. Inside the pocket of Paul's jacket, the officer found a small vial of hash oil. Paul was convicted for possession of marijuana and concentrated cannabis.

If Paul had known the law, he would have known that he should never throw marijuana down on the ground when he is the only person in the area, and a police officer is nearby. Paul's best move would have been to quickly place the joint into an empty pocket and casually walk back into the bar. In that case, Officer Bacon would have simply seen a man smoking a cigarette outside a bar. Such observations would not have given the officer probable cause to search Paul, nor even a reasonable suspicion to stop and detain him.

In another case, police in Arizona received information that a man had sold marijuana to two out-of-town women and was driving them to the airport. The police observed the man helping the women carry two suitcases. When the suitcases were passed through the x-ray machine, the officers observed what appeared to be bricks of marijuana on the x-ray picture. The officers asked the defendant for consent to search the suitcases. The defendant replied that the suitcases were not his, but rather belonged to the women. The women likewise denied ownership of the suitcases, claiming they were taking them for a friend. The police seized the suitcases, opened them, and discovered a large amount of marijuana inside. The man was convicted of possessing marijuana for sale. The court held that the man had voluntarily abandoned the suitcases when he denied ownership. Accordingly, he had no right to complain that the warrantless seizure and search of the suitcases violated his reasonable expectation of privacy.

In a rather strange case, a man in Maryland was hospitalized because an overdose of hashish oil had leaked from balloons he had swallowed. While in a semiconscious state, the man had a bowel movement into a hospital bed pan. The police, without a warrant, looked through the man's excrement and removed several balloons containing hashish oil. The man was subsequently convicted of possession after the court found that he maintained no reasonable expectation of privacy in his excrement that had been deposited in a bed pan rather than in the privacy of his own bathroom at home. In effect, the court held that the man had abandoned his own excrement and hence a warrantless search and seizure was fully permissible under the Fourth Amendment!

In another case, a woman in Louisiana who had several marijuana joints in her purse became nervous and began to run as a police officer approached her. At one point, out of either anger or nervousness, the woman threw her purse at the officer. The court held that the officer's subsequent warrantless search of the purse, which lead to his discovering marijuana cigarettes, was entirely legal because the woman had legally abandoned the purse and its contents by throwing it at the officer.

The Marijuana Aroma: "The Plain-Smell Rule?"

THE distinctive aroma of marijuana, burning or not, is recognizable by much of the population. Additionally, most police officers are trained to recognize the odor. Therefore, under the laws of almost every state, an officer who detects the odor of marijuana has probable cause to search the person or place from which he believes the odor is emanating.

Note, however, that the courts have looked at the nature of the container from which the odor was emanating. Generally speaking, if the container was one that judges would consider private, such as a briefcase, the courts have required that the officer obtain a search warrant before searching, despite the detection of the marijuana odor. On the other hand, if the container is less private in the eyes of a judge (e.g., if it is such as a brown paper bag), the courts are more likely to allow a warrantless search.

As is explained in Chapter 5, most courts permit an officer to conduct a warrantless search of a car if the odor of marijuana is detected. However (as explained in Chapter 6), without exigent circumstances or consent to enter, an officer cannot conduct a warrantless search of a home simply because he can smell marijuana coming from inside.

The Marijuana Aroma and Dog Sniffs

THE Supreme Court, as well as most state courts, has held that using a dog to sniff luggage or persons suspected of possessing or transporting marijuana is not a "search" and for that reason does not require a search warrant or probable cause. This means that an officer with a marijuana-sniffing dog is entirely free to approach you with his dog and let it have a sniff. The Supreme Court has explained its reasons for permitting warrantless dog sniffs of containers such as luggage:

> We have affirmed that a person possesses a privacy interest in the contents of personal luggage that is protected by the Fourth Amendment. A "canine sniff" by a well-trained nar-cotics-detection dog, however, does not require opening the luggage. It does not expose noncontraband items that other-wise would remain hidden from public view, as does, for example, an officer's rummaging through the contents of luggage. Thus, the manner in which information is obtained

through this investigative technique is much less intrusive than a typical search. Moreover, the sniff discloses only the presence or absence of narcotics, a contraband item. Thus, despite the fact that the sniff tells the authorities something about the contents of the luggage, the information obtained is limited. This limited disclosure also ensures that the owner of the property is not subjected to the embarrassment and inconvenience entailed in less discriminate and more intrusive investigative methods . . . We are aware of no other investigative procedure that is so limited both in the manner in which the information is obtained and in the content of the information revealed by the procedure. Therefore, we conclude that the particular course of investigation that the agents intended to pursue here—exposure of respondent's luggage, which was located in a public place, to a trained canine— did not constitute a "search" within the meaning of the Fourth Amendment.

A citizen is, of course, under no obligation to allow this to happen. An approach by an officer with a dog is merely a contact, and as discussed earlier any person is absolutely free to walk away and avoid the officer and dog completely. As explained earlier, the officer can detain a person only if he has a reasonable suspicion based on objective facts that a person is involved in criminal activity.

As a final note, at least one state court (New York) has held that under the *state constitution*, the use of man's best friend to sniff for drugs *is* a "search" and hence may be conducted only pursuant to a warrant or under an exception to the warrant requirement.

Border Searches
(Fifth Exception to the Warrant Requirement)

BECAUSE the federal government has the authority to exclude aliens from the country, courts have granted law-enforcement agents broad powers to conduct searches at or near borders. In fact, the United States Supreme Court has held that an officer does *not* need a warrant, probable cause, or even reasonable suspicion to search you, your car, or your belongings at a border. Therefore, any time you cross a U.S. border, you in effect consent to a search. Most people are aware of this rule and plan accordingly.

Two aspects of border searches are not as well-known. First, the rule has been extended to allow the opening and search of mail coming into or out of the United States. The inspectors do not need a warrant, probable cause, or even a reasonable suspicion that the mail contains marijuana or another drug before opening it. As a practical matter, this is generally done only if the mail looks bulky, emits an odor, or in some other way indicates that it may contain marijuana.

Second, the definition of "border" has been expanded to include airports that receive nonstop flights from foreign countries. Therefore, if a person flies into any U.S. airport directly from a foreign country, that person is subject to a warrantless search even though he or she may be a thousand miles from the closest geographical border.

Exigent Circumstances
(Sixth Exception to the Warrant Requirement)

AN officer may conduct a warrantless search or seizure if "exigent circumstances" exist. Exigent circumstances were described by one court as "an emergency situation requiring swift action to prevent imminent danger to life or serious damage to property, or to forestall the imminent escape of a suspect or destruction of evidence." As the quote indicates, this exception to the warrant requirement is very broad. Courts created the rule out of fear that some emergency situations require immediate action by the police, and that such actions would be hindered if an officer had to first obtain a search warrant.

In fact, the exigent-circumstances exception to the warrant requirement is often applied in marijuana cases to justify an officer's warrantless search on the theory that if the officer had to delay his search to obtain a search warrant, the suspect would have either destroyed, moved, or sold the marijuana that the officer was going to search for. For example, in one case an officer suspected that a particular residence was in the process of being burglarized. He checked the residence's windows and front door, but saw no evidence of forced entry. He then decided to knock on the front door just to check that everything was all right. The resident of the home, Doug, came to the door and opened it a few inches. Out came the overwhelming smell of burning marijuana. When Doug saw that it was a police officer on his doorstep, he quickly tried to close his door.

The officer used his foot to block the door and gain entry to Doug's home. Once inside, the officer arrested Doug and his friend for possession of marijuana. A California court noted that in most cases an officer must have a warrant to enter a person's home. However, the court held that the officer's warrantless entry of Doug's home was legal under the exigent-circumstances exception to the warrant requirement. The court explained that the odor of burning marijuana is unmistakable by a trained officer and hence it established probable cause that Doug and any other occupant was in possession of marijuana. Given that Doug saw the officer when he opened the door, the officer's immediate warrantless entry of the home was necessary to prevent Doug from destroying the marijuana.

Attempting to Swallow Incriminating Evidence

It's relatively common for individuals in possession of illegal drugs to become terrified at the approach of a police officer and to attempt to dispose of evidence by swallowing the drug. Often the police officer will immediately attempt to force the person to spit out the contraband. As a general rule, police officers may reach into a person's mouth to recover evidence if there is probable cause to believe a crime is being committed. No warrant is required for such a search, because immediate police action is necessary in order to prevent the destruction of evidence. As stated by the California Supreme Court, "the mouth is not a 'sacred orifice' and there is no constitutional right to destroy or dispose of evidence."

The Fourth Amendment does require that police officers who attempt to remove contraband from a person's mouth act reasonably and use only as much force as is necessary to remove the object. In other words, the police may not use brutal or excessive force, or engage in a removal technique that "shocks the conscience." For example, in one case an officer who had been surveilling an apartment unit suspected of being a "drug house" observed Michael Jones leave the unit carrying a tiny toy balloon believed to contain heroin. When the officer approached, Michael panicked and attempted to swallow the balloon. The officer grabbed Michael's lower jaw and for ten or fifteen seconds applied pressure to Michael's jaw and throat in an attempt to prevent him from swallowing the balloon. As Michael was shoved to the ground, the balloon was expelled and was later found to contain heroin.

The court held that, "a suspect may not be choked or abused in order to force evidence from his person or to prevent its disposal by swallowing . . . . choking a man to extract evidence from his mouth violates due process." The

court rejected the prosecution's argument that a "reasonable amount of choking" is permissible. The court stated:

> California law . . . has not recognized distinctions in a degree
> of choking, but rather has drawn the line of illegality at
> choking . . . . When illegality is shown the law does not
> recognize degrees of illegality and inquire whether the conduct
> was grossly or only mildly illegal. No object that is forced
> from an accused by means of choking should ever be received
> in evidence.

After stating the above rule, the court held that the officer's application
of force to Michael's throat and lower jaw was indeed "choking," and hence
illegal. As a result, the balloon and its contents were excluded from evidence.

In another case, police officers tackled an amputee in a wheel chair,
after observing him place a "two-inch wad" of masking tape into his mouth.
After knocking the man out of his wheel chair, several officers grabbed the
man's chin and placed pressure on his neck to prevent him from swallowing
the wad. When the man refused to spit out the wad, another officer pushed his
Bic pen into the man's mouth and successfully pried the object out. The court
held that this action was *legal* because there was no evidence that the officers
attempted to choke the man.

Searches at School if You Are a Student (Seventh Exception to the Warrant Requirement)

If you are a student at a public school, it is important to understand that the
United States Supreme Court has reduced the level of protection you have
against searches conducted at school by a school official. The case in which the
Court created this exception involved a female student, referred to by the Court
as T.L.O, who was reported to have been smoking in the school bathroom in
violation of school rules. She was called into the principal's office and questioned
by the assistant principal. Although T.L.O. denied smoking, the assistant principal did not believe her.

The assistant principal reasoned that if T.L.O. did smoke, then she
probably carried the pack of cigarettes in her purse. Without any more evidence,
and without a search warrant, the assistant principal snatched her purse, opened
it, and found a pack of cigarettes. Along with the cigarettes, he also saw a

package of rolling papers, which he associated with marijuana use. Based on this evidence he emptied T.L.O.'s purse and carefully searched its contents. In among her personal belongings, he discovered additional evidence of T.L.O.'s use and possible sale of marijuana.

Clearly, had this been a search of an adult's purse by a government agent, the Court would have held that it was illegal, since it was not based on a warrant. However, because the search was of a child, and on school property by a school official, the Court created a special exception to the warrant requirement. This exception permits public-school officials to search students and their belongings, if the official has a reasonable belief that the student possesses contraband. Under this rule, school searches by teachers and principals will almost always be upheld as legal. Remember, however, what little protection this rule gives to public-school students is *not* available to students at private schools. Private-school officials are not constrained by the Fourth Amendment. Therefore, officials at private schools may legally search a student for *any* reason. Not even a reasonable suspicion is required.

Marijuana and Your Telephone

THE United States Supreme Court held that people are reasonable in expecting the contents of their telephone conversations to be private. For this reason, the Court has held that a police officer must obtain a search warrant in order to tap a person's phone. Unfortunately, there is one very big exception to this rule, which is often used in marijuana investigations. Specifically, no search warrant is needed if *one* party to the conversation agrees. This often occurs in marijuana cases when the police apprehend a small-time marijuana user and make a deal with him to give him a break if he assists them in catching his supplier. The police will often instruct the user to call his supplier and set up a buy. As part of the deal, the police will obtain the user's "consent" to tape the telephone conversation. The contents of the conversation will be used against the supplier.

Likewise, it is well known that telephone companies routinely monitor conversations to perform maintenance, to monitor employee performance, and to prevent fraud. If such monitoring results in the interception of a conversation concerning a marijuana crime, the company can disclose the intercepted comments to the police, despite the fact that the information was obtained without a search warrant. Remember, the Fourth Amendment does not protect you against searches by private people and/or private companies.

An additional exception to the search-warrant requirement concerns telephone communications involving pagers and cordless phones. These broadcasts are easily intercepted with a radio. Most courts hold that, because such conversations can be intercepted by almost anyone, and often are, a person has no reasonable expectation of privacy in such communications. Therefore, the police are free to listen in on them without the need of a warrant.

Similarly, the Supreme Court has held that police officers may use what's known as a "pen-register" without obtaining a search warrant. A pen-register is a device that records all the telephone numbers that are dialed from, or received by, a particular residence. In fact, the Court has held that installation of such a device is not a "search"; so the Fourth Amendment is inapplicable, and police can install such devices for any reason.

In the case that created this rule, the police suspected that Mr. Smith was involved in a robbery. The officers, without first obtaining a search warrant, attached a pen-register to Mr. Smith's telephone line at the central telephone office. The device recorded every number dialed into and out of Mr. Smith's home, and in so doing, provided some incriminating evidence against Mr. Smith.

At a pretrial hearing, Mr. Smith asked the court to exclude all evidence derived from the pen-register, arguing that it was a warrantless search and unreasonable under the Fourth Amendment. The case went all the way to the Supreme Court, which held that installation of the pen-register was not a "search." The Court reasoned that because the pen-register was installed at the phone company, Smith could not claim that his property was invaded or that the police intruded into a "constitutionally protected area." The Court rejected Smith's argument that the pen-register infringed on his legitimate right of privacy. The Court explained that the register recorded only the numbers dialed and not the contents of his conversation. The Court reasoned that telephone users realize that such information is available for use by the phone company in determining the subscriber's monthly bill, and hence subscribers have no reasonable expectation of privacy in the information. For these reasons, no warrant is required before law enforcement officers install a pen-register.

Marijuana and the Mail

THE law concerning marijuana and the mail is similar to that regarding the government's eavesdropping on your telephone conversations. Like the contents of a telephone conversation, the contents of a letter or package is considered private by most reasonable people. The Supreme Court has held that United

States *first-class* mail, whether a letter or package, is protected by the Fourth Amendment. Therefore, the government cannot open first-class mail on the mere hunch that it contains marijuana. Rather, the government must obtain a search warrant based on probable cause that marijuana will be found inside the letter or package.

A government agent's failure to obtain a search warrant before opening first-class mail will result in the exclusion from court of any marijuana found during such an illegal mail search. Remember, however, only first-class mail is protected. Mail sent other than first class does not receive the same stringent protection. Moreover, mail sent through a *private* mail carrier, such as Federal Express or United Parcel Service, receives *no* protection under the Fourth Amendment if opened by employees of the private carrier. To repeat, the Fourth Amendment protects you against unreasonable searches *only* by the government or its agents—there is no protection against searches by private people.

One exception to the rule concerning the first-class U.S. mail applies to mail that is mailed from outside the United States with a destination inside the United States. The courts have held that the border exception to the warrant requirement allows government agents to open first-class mail if they suspect, for any reason, that it contains marijuana or other drugs. No warrant is required for such a search.

Lastly, with respect to mail, this rule is parallel to that for telephone pen-registers. Specifically, the United States Supreme Court has held that you have no reasonable expectations of privacy in the information contained on the *outside* of your mail. For this reason, the courts have held that the police may conduct "mail covers" without the need for a warrant, probable cause, or even a reasonable suspicion. During a mail cover, the police record the addresses of everyone you send mail to and everyone you receive mail from. This information can be used against you if the police find that you sent or received mail from another person who is a known marijuana grower or user.

5. Marijuana & Your Car

When Can a Police Officer Stop Your Car?

A very large proportion of marijuana arrests occur in conjunction with traffic stops. An officer can pull over a vehicle if he has a *reasonable suspicion* that the driver or occupant committed a crime or traffic violation. There are numerous court cases in which people were convicted of marijuana crimes following an officer's stop of their vehicle due to: double parking, expired registration tags, speeding, dirty windshield that obstructed the driver's view, faulty muffler, smoking car, driving over a double line, no registration tag, headlights out, broken tail light, failure to dim high beams, no brake lights, no license plate, illegible license plate, unsafe lane change, weaving, no rear plate light, and bald tires. If your car has any such defects, or if you violate any traffic laws, you are inviting a police officer to pull you over at any time.

Roadblocks (Second Exception to the Reasonable-Suspicion Rule)

In general, an officer must have reasonable suspicion (see Chapter 3) in order to legally pull over a person driving a vehicle. However, the Supreme Court has created an exception to this rule for roadblocks. Currently, the most common use of roadblocks is to detect and deter drunk drivers. When the police properly conduct such a roadblock, they may stop vehicles without any reason to believe that the driver is under the influence. However, once the vehicle is stopped, the officers must quickly allow the driver to pass through unless they observe facts that create a reasonable suspicion that the driver is intoxicated or otherwise violating the law.

In other words, a police roadblock allows the officers *only* to stop your vehicle. They cannot search you or your car without probable cause to believe that you are violating the law. Likewise, you retain every right to refuse to consent to an officer's request to search.

Ordering You Out of Your Car

ONCE a police officer legally stops a vehicle, he has the right to order the driver to get out of the car. This is a routine procedure which most courts have allowed for officer safety reasons. Upon ordering a person out, the officer may conduct a pat-search of the person's outer clothing only if he sees a bulge or has some other reasonable basis for believing the person is armed or dangerous.

In a handful of states the officer can also order a passenger to get out. In every state, the officer can order a passenger out if the officer has a reasonable belief that the passenger may pose a danger, or if it is reasonably necessary in order for the officer to complete his investigation.

When Can a Police Officer Search Your Car?

THERE are several things that can trigger an officer's right to search your car without a warrant. Specifically, an officer can conduct a warrantless search of your car if you are legally stopped and:

1. the officer reasonably believes you may have a weapon in the vehicle; *or*
2. the officer has probable cause to believe there is marijuana inside the car; *or*
3. the officer arrests you; *or*
4. your car is impounded.

Vehicle Search for Officer Safety

AS noted above, if a police officer legally stops a vehicle and reasonably believes an occupant may be dangerous or armed with a weapon, the officer can order the occupant out of the car, and search the passenger compartment of the vehicle for weapons.

In one famous case, police officers, on patrol late at night, observed a car speeding and weaving. As they watched, the driver of the car lost control and swerved into a ditch. When the officers got to the car, the driver, Mr. Long, was already out of the car. He exhibited all the classic symptoms of intoxication. When the officers asked to see his vehicle registration, Mr. Long walked back to his car to retrieve it. At that moment, the officers saw a large hunting knife on the floor board of his car and immediately ordered him to freeze. They pat-searched Mr. Long but found no weapons. The officers then directed their flashlights inside the car to look for any other weapons in plain view. Although they saw no weapons, they did see a large open pouch in the front seat. The pouch appeared to contain a large amount of marijuana. Based on their observations, the officers arrested Mr. Long for possession of marijuana, and after searching the car found 75 pounds of marijuana.

The Court concluded that the officers acted constitutionally when they looked into Mr. Long's car with their flashlights. The Court explained that even when a suspect has been removed from his vehicle for questioning, the police may still conduct a "protective search" of the vehicle's interior. The Court reasoned that a suspect might break away and enter his vehicle, thereby obtaining a hidden weapon. In addition, the Court explained, if a suspect is not arrested following a detention, he will be allowed to return to his car and could retrieve a weapon at that time. Therefore, for "officer safety reasons," whenever a police officer reasonably believes a suspect may be dangerous, the officer can search the passenger compartment of the suspect's vehicle. Moreover, when such a search for weapons is conducted, the officers may seize any illegal drugs found during the search.

Vehicle Searches Based on Probable Cause (The Second Exception to the Warrant Requirement)

ALTHOUGH a police officer can stop your vehicle with only a reasonable suspicion of criminal activity, he cannot typically search your vehicle unless he has probable cause to believe you are or were engaged in criminal activity. In other words, if a police officer stops you for speeding, he ordinarily cannot search your car. However, if an officer stops your car, and if in some way probable cause develops that there is marijuana in the vehicle, the Supreme Court has held that the officer can immediately conduct a warrantless search of you and your vehicle's passenger compartment.

Probable Cause: Marijuana Odor, Hand-Rolled Cigarettes, Cannabis Seeds, & Roach Clips

THERE are thousands of cases in which officers stopped a vehicle for a minor traffic violation, but ended up arresting the driver or occupants because probable cause developed that marijuana was inside the car. In one case in Arizona, the officers stopped Mr. Lynch's vehicle for reckless driving. Mr. Lynch told the officer that his driver's license was in his shirt pocket. When the officer reached into the car to retrieve the license, he detected the odor of fresh marijuana. Without obtaining a warrant, the officer searched Lynch's vehicle, discovering marijuana, hashish, and some pipes. The Arizona court upheld the warrantless search, holding that the odor of marijuana provided probable cause that Lynch was in the process of transporting marijuana in his vehicle.

After Nebraska police officers stopped Mr. Daly's truck for speeding, one officer detected a "faint odor of marijuana" that seemed stronger near the back of the truck. The officer advised Mr. Daly of the odor and "requested" that Mr. Daly open the rear door of the truck. Mr. Daly complied, the officer smelled the strong odor of marijuana, and proceeded to search the truck without a warrant. Inside the truck, the officer found more than 500 pounds of marijuana. The Nebraska court upheld the officer's warrantless search, finding that the officer had made approximately 50 similar arrests in the past after detecting the odor of marijuana. Therefore, given the officer's special training and experience, his detection of the marijuana odor gave him probable cause to believe that Daly's vehicle contained marijuana.

Occasionally the courts have held that an officer's detection of a marijuana odor is *not* sufficient to establish probable cause for a warrantless search of the vehicle. However, in those cases it was either because the officer simply lacked experience or training to positively identify the odor as marijuana, or because the source of the odor could not be pinpointed or its "freshness" determined.

For example, after Michigan state police officers had legally stopped Mr. Hilber's car, one officer detected the odor of burnt marijuana emanating from the vehicle. For that reason, the officer performed a warrantless search of the vehicle, recovering marijuana and other drugs. The Michigan court held that the officer's warrantless search was illegal, because the odor alone did not establish probable cause. The court based its holding on the fact that the officer had no training in determining how long the odor of marijuana can linger. Therefore the officer could not reasonably infer that the driver had just been smoking marijuana or that the car contained marijuana.

In a similar case in Montana, a court refused to find probable cause for a warrantless vehicle search after an officer detected a combined odor of incense and marijuana following a vehicle stop. The court referred to the officer's own testimony that the odor of marijuana can linger in a vehicle for more than a day. Therefore, because the officer did not actually see the vehicle's occupants smoking, or observe any other evidence of marijuana, the odor alone was insufficient to establish a probable cause that the vehicle currently contained marijuana.

The Supreme Court of New Hampshire has held that an officer's observation of a hand-rolled cigarette, without more, was insufficient evidence of marijuana use to entitle the officer to reach into a vehicle and retrieve the hand-rolled cigarette without a warrant. In that case, New Hampshire state troopers stopped a vehicle driven by Forrest Ball. As one trooper approached the vehicle, he "observed several partially smoked manufactured cigarettes, as well as a partially smoked hand-rolled cigarette, in an ashtray located on the top of the dashboard. Unable to identify the contents of the hand-rolled cigarette by sight, the officer reached in, removed it from the ashtray and smelled it. He determined that the cigarette contained marijuana, and the defendant was placed under arrest. They searched the defendant's person which led to the discovery of additional contraband." The New Hampshire Supreme Court held that the officer's warrantless seizure of the hand-rolled cigarette was illegal, even under the plain-view rule, because the incriminating nature of the cigarette was not immediately apparent. The court stated:

> not all hand-rolled cigarettes contain contraband. Consequently, we cannot say that observation of a hand-rolled cigarette, by itself, would lead a reasonable and prudent person to believe that the cigarette contained an illegal substance. To transfer a mere suspicion about the contents of the hand-rolled cigarette into a reasonable belief based on probable cause, the officer must articulate additional collaborating facts. For instance, it might be shown that the arresting officer had the ability to distinguish hand-rolled marijuana and tobacco cigarettes by sight, or that he perceived the odor of marijuana, or that the defendant made a furtive gesture in an attempt to conceal the cigarette, or that the defendant's conduct was otherwise incriminating.

After stopping a vehicle driven by Julian Franklin, a New York state police officer observed a roach clip on Julian's key ring, which had a "charred residue" on the end but did not hold the remnants of a joint. After observing the roach clip, the officer conducted a warrantless search of Julian's car and discovered several plastic baggies of marijuana. The New York court held that the officer's observation of the roach clip did not give rise to probable cause to search Julian's car. Why? Because the officer "had no indication that the roach clip had recently been used for smoking marijuana by reason of its being hot or by the presence of smoke in the vehicle." Therefore, the court dismissed the case against Julian because the officer's illegal search resulted in the exclusion of all the evidence.

In many states, any amount of marijuana seen in a car establishes probable cause to search the car's interior. In one case, officers stopped a car and spotted a single seed and a few stems on the back seat. The court held that was sufficient to permit the officers to search the car's passenger compartment.

In another case, Officers Moffett and Najera were on routine patrol when they observed a vehicle speeding and occasionally swerving out of its lane. The officers stopped the vehicle for speeding, suspecting that the driver might be tired or under the influence. Officer Najera approached the vehicle and spoke with the driver, Steven Wimberly. Officer Moffett approached the passenger side, where Richard Harrison was seated. As he approached, Moffett shined his flashlight into the vehicle and saw, among other things, a smoking pipe and twelve dark seeds on the floor near Richard's feet.

The general characteristics of the seeds, coupled with their proximity to the pipe, led Moffett to conclude they were Cannabis seeds. Moffett ordered Richard to hand him the pipe, and Richard complied. The officer sniffed the pipe, detecting the odor of burnt marijuana. He also observed a burnt residue, including some seeds and stems, inside the pipe.

At this point, the officers ordered Richard and Steven to get out of the car, and searched the car. Inside, they detected the odor of burnt marijuana. Additionally, inside the pocket of a jacket found in the car, Officer Moffett found a plastic bag containing a small amount of marijuana. The officers then used Steven's keys to open the vehicle's trunk. Inside the trunk, they found a suitcase, which they proceeded to open, revealing several pounds of marijuana and hashish.

The California Supreme Court held that Officer Moffett's search of the vehicle's passenger compartment was legal. The Court explained that Moffett had probable cause based on his observation of the pipe and the seeds. The Court pointed out that Moffett's observation of the seeds alone was sufficient to establish probable cause to search the vehicle's passenger compartment as well as any container within the compartment such as the jacket. Therefore all the evidence found in the car's passenger compartment was admissible against Steven and Richard.

The Court then went on, however, to hold that the officer's search of the vehicle's *trunk* was *illegal*. The Court explained that the officer's discovery of the pipe, seeds, and small bag of marijuana was indicative of the casual use of marijuana. Nothing indicated that the two men were transporting marijuana in the trunk. In other words, although there was probable cause to search the passenger compartment, the officer's further intrusion into the vehicle's trunk was unlawful because there was no probable cause that marijuana would be found therein. As a result, the Court held that the large amount of marijuana and hashish found in the trunk was inadmissible in court.

Unlike a vehicle's passenger compartment, which is surrounded by see-through windows, a vehicle's trunk normally cannot be seen into from outside. Accordingly, the courts have found that it is reasonable for a person to expect more privacy in the contents of a vehicle's trunk than in the vehicle's passenger compartment. For this reason, as can be seen in the case of Steven and Richard, the rule has developed that probable cause to search a vehicle's passenger compartment may not be enough to justify the search of the vehicle's trunk. Rather, in order for an officer without a warrant to search the trunk of a vehicle for marijuana, he must have probable cause to believe that marijuana is concealed *in the trunk*.

In one case, probable cause to search the trunk was held to exist when a vehicle attempted to outrun the police; when it was subsequently stopped, a kilo of marijuana was seen in plain view on the back seat and three joints on the floorboard. The court held that, given the plain-view observations coupled with the desperate attempts to avoid apprehension, the officers had probable cause to believe the occupants were transporting a large amount of contraband in their vehicle. Therefore the trunk search was legal.

In another case, officers stopped a vehicle and discovered a baggie of marijuana in the passenger compartment. In addition, the officers smelled a very strong odor of fresh, unburned marijuana that could not be attributed to the baggie. The court held that this gave the officers probable cause to believe that additional marijuana was in the trunk.

One court nicely summarized the rule for probable cause to search a vehicle's passenger compartment versus probable cause to search a vehicle's trunk compartment:

The lawful observation of marijuana debris on a seat or the floor of the interior of the car, or in the clothing of the occupants, or the smell of burned marijuana emanating from the interior of the car would give probable cause to believe that marijuana might be found in the areas adjacent and immediately accessible to the occupants, such as ashtrays, a passenger console, a glove compartment and underneath and between the seats . . . . Similarly, if a substantial quantity of marijuana is found inside the automobile or on the person of an occupant, it reasonably may be inferred that additional contraband may be concealed in areas of the car not immediately accessible and adjacent to the occupants, such as the trunk or under the hood. A substantial quantity of marijuana in the interior of the car would give rise to a logical inference that the car was being used to transport marijuana.

Breaking Open Your Vehicle's Trunk

As the above cases indicate, it is often possible for officers to have probable cause to search a vehicle's passenger compartment, but no probable cause to search the vehicle's trunk. Often, in such cases, the officers will put lots of pressure on the person to consent to a search of the vehicle's trunk. Obviously, if you find yourself in such a situation, and have a large amount of marijuana in your trunk, you should *not* consent to the search. However, be prepared for the fact that the officers will likely open the trunk anyway in hopes that a court will later find that they did have probable cause to believe it contained marijuana.

On the other hand, if the officers find some marijuana in the passenger compartment and you *know* that you have none in the trunk, then there is no harm in consenting to the search of your trunk. As mentioned above, it is quite likely the officers will search your trunk even without your consent in the hopes that a court will find they had probable cause to do so. In such a situation, if you do not consent, the officers will likely cause some severe and costly damage to your car by breaking open the trunk.

As one court explained:

If the officers have the right to engage in a warrantless search of the entire car they may do so by any means reasonably available; thus, if the trunk key cannot be located they may break open the trunk. Carried to its logical end, if the officers have the right to search the entire car and it is necessary to accomplish their purpose, they may rip apart any part of the car in which they should suspect that additional contraband may be found.

Therefore, if you *know* you have nothing illegal in the trunk, it is often in your financial interest to open your trunk and let the officer have a look.

Vehicle Searches Incident to Arrest

THE United States Supreme Court has held that any time a police officer legally arrests a person in an automobile, the officer can legally search the person as well as the entire passenger compartment of the vehicle. Moreover, the officer's search can include the opening of closed containers found inside the passenger compartment.

In the case in which the Supreme Court created this rule, Officer Nicot, a New York State police officer, was driving an unmarked police car when he was passed by a speeding car. Officer Nicot gave chase and pulled the vehicle over. Inside were four occupants, including Roger Belton, who was seated in the back seat.

When Officer Nicot approached the car to write a speeding ticket, he smelled the odor of burnt marijuana. In addition, as he spoke with the driver, he noticed an envelope on the floorboard of the car marked, "Supergold." In the officer's experience, such factors added up to probable cause that marijuana was inside the envelope and that the occupants had been smoking marijuana as they drove.

Therefore, under the New York law that presumes all persons in a car to be in possession of any marijuana found in the passenger compartment, Officer Nicot ordered all four occupants out of the car and arrested them for possession of marijuana. Then, incident to the arrest of the men, the officer picked up the envelope and found that it did indeed contain marijuana. The officer searched the entire passenger compartment of the vehicle. On the back seat, where Roger Belton had been sitting, Officer Nicot found a black leather jacket. He unzipped the jacket's pockets and inside found additional illegal drugs. Roger was subsequently convicted of possessing narcotics.

Roger argued his case all the way to the Supreme Court. His position was that the officer had no right to search the closed pocket of his jacket without a search warrant. Roger argued that because Officer Nicot failed to get a search warrant, the search was illegal; hence all evidence of drugs found in the jacket should be excluded from court.

Needless to say, the Supreme Court disagreed with Roger. The Court held that any time a police officer makes a legal arrest of a person in a car, the officer automatically has the right to immediately search the passenger compartment of the car. Moreover, the officer may open and look inside any containers that he finds inside the passenger compartment. The Court broadly defined "containers" as:

> any object capable of holding another object. It thus includes closed or open glove compartments, consoles, or other receptacles located anywhere within the passenger compartment, as well as luggage, boxes, bags, clothing, and the like.

The Court did place one very important limit on the vehicle search, stating that the arrest of a vehicle's occupant does *not*, by itself, permit the police to search the vehicle's *trunk*. Therefore an officer's arrest of a vehicle's occupant allows him to search the vehicle's passenger compartment, but not the vehicle's trunk, unless, he has probable cause to believe that marijuana is inside the trunk.

Throwing Marijuana from a Moving Vehicle

As discussed earlier, a person retains no reasonable expectation of privacy in abandoned property. For that reason, the person cannot complain of an officer's warrantless search or seizure of the property once it has been abandoned.

In one case, narcotics officers received a tip that a man would be transferring some marijuana from his home into his truck. The officers staked out the man's home and just on schedule, observed the man exit the home with a package and place it in the truck. The man then got in the truck and drove away. One of the officers tried to pull the truck over by driving alongside the truck and flashing the man his police badge. However, rather than pull over, the man accelerated and the agents gave chase. During the chase, the man tossed out the window the package that the officers had earlier seen the man place in the truck. The officers recovered the package, searched it without a warrant, and discovered the marijuana.

The court held that because the man abandoned the package, the officer's retrieval and discovery of the marijuana inside the package was neither a "search" or a "seizure." Therefore the officers warrantless search of the package was entirely legal under the Fourth Amendment.

In another case, police officers performing a routine traffic stop of a speeding vehicle observed the passenger toss a bag out the window. The police recovered the bag and found marijuana inside. The court upheld the passenger's conviction for possessing marijuana, noting that if the passenger had not been so stupid as to toss the marijuana out the window, it would likely never have been found, because the officers would have been unable to search the vehicle given that the stop was merely for speeding.

Automobile Inventory & Impound Searches

MANY times when a person is arrested following a vehicle stop, the arresting officer will have the person's car towed away and impounded. This is often done when the driver is alone and is arrested after his vehicle is stopped on a public street.

Any time your car is impounded by the police, most states permit the police to "inventory" the contents of your vehicle to avoid a lawsuit in which you might claim items were not returned to you. This is known as an "inventory search." The scope of an inventory search is very broad. In most states, the police can open a vehicle's *trunk* and inventory closed containers found anywhere in the car. Therefore a vehicle impound search is even broader than the search permitted incident to the arrest of a vehicle's occupant.

In one case that went all the way to the United States Supreme Court, a Florida Highway Patrol trooper stopped Martin Well's vehicle for speeding. After smelling alcohol on Martin's breath, the trooper arrested him for driving under the influence of alcohol and impounded his vehicle. At the impound facility, an inventory search turned up "two marijuana cigarette butts in an ashtray and a locked suitcase in the trunk." The police forced open the suitcase and discovered a garbage bag containing marijuana.

The Supreme Court upheld the warrantless search of the ashtray, trunk, and suitcase, noting that the search was reasonable in order "to protect an owner's property while it is in the custody of the police, to insure against claims of lost, stolen, or vandalized property, and to guard the police from danger."

In another case, a man named Bill had grown a very robust Cannabis plant inside the closet of his city apartment. However, because of the plant's rapidly increasing size and aroma, Bill decided he and the plant would be better off if he moved it to the backyard of his secluded summer cabin in the country. One night, Bill carefully covered the plant with a bed sheet and quietly carried it outside to his van. Bill then began the long drive to his cabin.

Along the way, Bill stopped at his favorite restaurant and had dinner. As he left the restaurant he was mortified to see that his van was gone. After running around the parking lot in a panic, he came to the realization that he had mistakenly parked in a "No Parking" zone and the police had towed his van. When Bill arrived at the police impound lot, he was arrested on numerous marijuana charges, including cultivation, transporting, and possession.

Bill did everything right except for parking in a "No Parking" zone. Since the police impounded his van, they were legally able to conduct an inventory search which revealed the Cannabis plant.

Since an inventory search is permitted only if your car is impounded, it stands to reason that you can avoid such a search if you can prevent the officer from impounding your car. There are several ways you can try doing this. First, if you have a passenger in the car when you are arrested, and that person is legally able to drive, you can try turning your keys over to the passenger and giving him or her permission to drive your car home for you.

Second, some people have been able to appeal to the officer's goodwill by being very polite during the arrest and then asking the officer if he would be so kind as to move the vehicle off the road and into a private parking lot. (Obviously, you do not want to use this tactic if you think the officer will smell or see marijuana when he enters your car.) Some officers understand that impounding a vehicle costs the owner a lot of money, and if you can get them to sympathize with you, they may move your vehicle to give you a break.

Lastly, you may be able to avoid impoundment if you yourself pull your vehicle into a private parking lot. If you suddenly realize that an officer is pulling you over, and you suspect you are going to be arrested, you should immediately look for an upcoming parking lot to pull into. The goal is to get your car off the public roadway, thereby making it much less likely that the officer will have it impounded. Of course, you must be very careful when using this tactic. If you drive too far after the officer turns on his overhead lights or siren, you could face an additional charge of fleeing a police officer.

A Recent Supreme Court Decision Concerning Containers in Automobiles

In May of 1991, the United States Supreme Court created a new rule that severely reduced a person's right to privacy in closed containers taken into an automobile. In this case, Officer Coleman of the Santa Ana, California, Police Department, received word from a D.E.A. agent that they had intercepted a package of marijuana that was addressed to a person in Santa Ana. Officer Coleman was told to take the package to the local Federal Express office and secretly wait for the addressee to come and claim the package. Officer Coleman did so, and observed a person retrieve the package. Officer Coleman followed the person to his home and staked out the house with several other officers.

After a few hours, the officers observed another individual (later identified as Steven) arrive at the home. Steven left about ten minutes after arriving, and carried a brown paper bag that was the same size as the marijuana package sent through the mail. Steven placed the bag in the trunk of his car and drove away. The officers followed him, stopped him, opened the trunk, opened the bag, and found marijuana inside. Steven was arrested.

At his trial in California, Steven's attorney successfully argued that the officers' search of the bag was illegal, because the officers failed to get a search warrant for the trunk or the bag. The United States Supreme Court disagreed, holding that the officers' search was legal.

The strangeness of this decision should be clear to you if you recall what was explained earlier regarding search warrants. To review, if an officer sees a person walking down the street with a closed container such as a briefcase, and has probable cause to believe the briefcase contains marijuana, he cannot open the briefcase without first obtaining a search warrant (unless, of course, the person consents to the warrantless search, or another exception to the warrant requirement applies). He must get a search warrant even if he has probable cause to believe that the container contains marijuana.

However, under the new law created by the Supreme Court, if you get into a car, carrying that same briefcase, an officer magically is able to search the container *without* first getting a search warrant! Therefore the bottom line is that once a container is placed in an automobile, it loses a great deal of its protection against warrantless searches.

Your Car and the Plain-View Rule

If a police officer has stopped your vehicle for a valid reason, he can seize any objects which he sees in plain view so long as their illegal nature is immediately apparent. A common example of the plain-view rule in action arises when a person is stopped for a simple traffic violation. When the officer comes up to write the traffic ticket, he sees some marijuana on the dashboard or in the ashtray. In such cases, it is not an illegal search or seizure for the officer to reach into the car and seize the marijuana without first obtaining a warrant. As explained earlier, the automobile exception to the warrant requirement allows an officer to conduct a warrantless search of a vehicle so long as he has probable cause to believe that it contains marijuana. Any marijuana found can, and will, be used against the person in court.

Furtive Movements

A recurring issue in many auto searches is what has come to be know as "furtive movements." A furtive movement is one that looks as if a person is attempting to retrieve or conceal a weapon, for example, an officer pulls a person over, for lawful reasons, and sees an occupant bend down or reach behind the seat.

Occasionally, when an officer performs a search of a vehicle that he later believes may have been illegal, he will try to beef up his report by indicating that "the suspect made a furtive movement as if he was retrieving a weapon," or "as I pulled over the suspect's vehicle, I observed him bend down as if to retrieve a weapon from under his seat."

As was previously explained, a police officer ordinarily can't search a vehicle or its occupants following a routine traffic violation. However, if the officer sees the driver or occupant make a furtive movement, the officer has a legitimate concern for his safety and is therefore permitted to search the area into which he saw the person reach. Moreover, if some other factor, in combination with the person's furtive movement, gives the officer probable cause to believe the person is transporting marijuana, the officer has a right to arrest the person and search the entire passenger compartment of the car, including closed containers.

Note: a furtive gesture alone does not constitute probable cause of criminal activity and hence almost every court would find that a general vehicle search based only on a furtive movement is illegal. However, it is always good advice to avoid making any movement that an officer might consider furtive. Such movements are often the straw that turns what would have been an illegal search into a lawful search.

Consenting to a Search of Your Car and Withdrawing Consent

IF a police officer is unable to establish probable cause for a search of a car, he can still search if the car's driver gives consent. The officer will usually say something like, "Would you please open your trunk?" or, "Do you mind if I look in your trunk?" Remember, as explained earlier, the officer is hoping the person will foolishly waive his or her constitutional right to be free from unreasonable searches. In this situation, a person desiring to assert his constitutional right to be free from unreasonable searches and seizures is wise to politely withhold consent and to inform the officer he would like to continue on his way. If for some reason the person does consent to a search, he may withdraw his consent if he does it before the officer finds something illegal.

As an example, Officer Friday legally stopped Ernie's car because of its cracked windshield. Friday had a hunch that Ernie was a marijuana smoker, but had no probable cause to search his car. Therefore Friday asked Ernie, "Would you mind if I looked in your trunk?" Ernie, not wanting to offend the nice officer, handed Friday the key to his trunk and stepped out of his way. Friday opened the trunk and began searching.

Suddenly Ernie remembered that he had a small bag of marijuana inside the first-aid kit in his trunk. Ernie quickly but calmly told Officer Friday, "O.K., stop your search. That's good enough. I've gotta get going now."

Analysis: Ernie was foolish to consent to the trunk search. However, withdrawal of his consent was valid, since Officer Friday had not yet found anything illegal. If Officer Friday had continued searching after Ernie withdrew his consent, any marijuana found should have been excluded from court.

Whose Pot Is It?

IF the police find marijuana hidden in your car (rather than on one of the passengers), a presumption arises that the marijuana was possessed by you because you control the vehicle. In most states, a passenger in a vehicle is not presumed to be in control of the vehicle, and hence is rarely convicted of possession when marijuana is discovered hidden in a car. To convict a passenger in such cases, the prosecution must produce evidence that links the passenger with the marijuana.

In one case, Texas police officers stopped a car and discovered more than 400 pounds of marijuana in the vehicle's trunk. The driver, as well as the passenger, Lawrence McCullough, were arrested and subsequently convicted of possessing marijuana. They each received a five-year sentence in state prison. Lawrence appealed his conviction, arguing that he was simply a passenger in the car and that the evidence was insufficient to prove that he knew that marijuana was inside the vehicle's trunk. The prosecutor argued that the arresting officer smelled marijuana inside the car and that so must have Lawrence. The officer also observed the vehicle's spare tire in the back seat, which gave him, as well as Lawrence, reason to believe that something was inside the trunk. Lastly, the prosecutor argued that the officer noted that Lawrence "was nervous, with a rapid heartbeat, breathing heavily, and appeared to be excited and trembling."

The court found that these factors were insufficient to convict a passenger of possessing marijuana found inside a vehicle's trunk. Why? Because the court agreed with Lawrence's arguments that the fact that trained police officers could smell marijuana is no evidence that he could do so; that the items in the back seat failed to prove that he knew marijuana was in the trunk; and that nervousness is an appropriate response to a confrontation with police officers and did not necessarily indicate Lawrence knew there was marijuana in the trunk.

Note that a trend may be starting in the other direction, initiated by a New York law that any drugs found in a car (except those found on an occupant) are presumed to be possessed by each and every person in the car at the time the drug was found! This is an extremely harsh law which permits the prosecutor to get several convictions where before he would likely have gotten one. Under the New York law, every occupant must prove his or her innocence if marijuana is found in the passenger compartment.

Driving Under the Influence of Marijuana

IN every state, it is a crime to "drive" or "operate" a motor vehicle while under the influence of marijuana. There are basically two elements to the crime: (1) driving or operating a motor vehicle, and (2) being under the influence of marijuana at the time of such driving.

The various states differ in the precise action outlawed. At last count, seven states make it illegal to "drive" a motor vehicle while under the influence. In these states, the courts originally interpreted the word "drive" as requiring actual *movement* of the vehicle. However, the recent trend is to broaden the crime of "driving" under the influence; hence some courts have interpreted "drive" to be the same as "operate." Therefore the difference between the two types of laws is really insignificant, because nearly all those states which outlaw "driving" under the influence are now broadly interpreting that word to include simply "operating" a motor vehicle.

Those states which outlaw "operating" a vehicle when under the influence interpret their law more broadly than for "driving." In most such states, "operating" is often defined as simply having access to the physical controls of the vehicle. A very good and surprisingly common example of the long arm of this law is that which occurred to Gene.

Gene, a constant marijuana smoker, was on a solo road trip on a relatively unused state route. As midnight approached, he decided to pull off the road, onto the shoulder, and sleep a few hours. He turned off his headlights as well as his engine. However, because it was rather chilly outside, he left his keys in the ignition and turned them to the position that would allow him to run his heater and listen to the radio.

As Gene was drifting off to sleep, he was awakened by bright headlights directly behind him. When he peeked out his back window, he was greeted by the local sheriff, who was stopping just to see if Gene needed some assistance. When Gene rolled down his window to speak with the sheriff, the sheriff smelled marijuana and, after giving Gene some field sobriety tests, arrested Gene for operating a motor vehicle while under the influence of marijuana.

Gene's attorney argued that Gene's action did not constitute "operating" a vehicle. Needless to say, the court disagreed. The court held that Gene was indeed "operating" the vehicle by placing his keys in its ignition and turning on the electrical components. Therefore Gene's conviction for driving under the influence of marijuana was upheld.

The states are split on the issue of whether a crime is committed if the driving or operating of a vehicle occurred only on *private* property. In some states, the law explicitly states that the conduct is only outlawed "on a *public* highway." However, the clear trend is to outlaw *any* driving under the influence, whether on public or on private property. California has just such a law, representative of the recent trend, which states: "It is unlawful for any person who is under the influence of an alcoholic beverage or any drug, or when under the combined influence of an alcoholic beverage and any drug, to drive a vehicle."

Under such a law, it is clear that a person can be arrested and convicted of driving under the influence when backing out of his driveway, driving a tractor on farm lands, or driving in a private parking lot.

If a police officer has reason to believe you are driving under the influence of *any* drug (including legal drugs), he can stop your vehicle and require you to take some roadside sobriety tests. These tests involve physical tests, such as walking heel-to-toe, touching your nose, and balancing on one foot, as well as mental tests, such as counting backward.

In addition to giving you these tests, an officer who suspects you of driving under the influence of marijuana will likely shine his flashlight in your eyes, measure the responsiveness of your pupils, and take your pulse. After the officer administers any or all of these tests, he can arrest you if your poor performance gives him probable cause to believe that you were driving or operating a vehicle under the influence of marijuana.

Often, the real proof that a person was "under the influence" of marijuana comes by way of a blood or urine test. In most states, any person who applies for and receives a driver's license impliedly consents to submit to a breath, blood, or urine test if an officer reasonably suspects him or her of driving under the influence of alcohol or a drug. However, because most breath-testing machines cannot detect marijuana, most state laws require a person suspected of driving under the influence of marijuana to take a blood or urine test, as opposed to a breath test. In California, the penalty for refusing to take such a test is an automatic, minimum one-year suspension of the person's driving privilege.

If you take a blood or urine test and marijuana is detected, the prosecution will introduce the results of that test into evidence, and have an expert testify that the level of marijuana in your blood or urine was sufficient to impair your driving ability to an appreciable degree. Your attorney may be able to counter this argument by presenting other expert testimony or by cross-examining the prosecution's expert.

In addition, if you are ever charged with driving under the influence of marijuana, you should advise your attorney of a little-known study conducted by the California Highway Patrol. In this study, the CHP tested the correlation between marijuana smoking and a person's ability to competently operate their vehicle. To the CHP's surprise and despair, they discovered that some people actually drive *better* after smoking marijuana! The study is reported in an article titled "Marijuana and Alcohol: A Driver Performance Study—A Final Report." It was published in 1986 by the California Department of Justice.

6. Marijuana & Your Home

A Home Is Entitled to Maximum Protection

SINCE the beginning of our country, the Supreme Court has held that a person is reasonably entitled to the highest degree of privacy when inside his or her home. An excerpt from a recent opinion by the Court makes it very clear that the Court is prepared to severely scrutinize all searches and seizures that occur inside a person's home:

> The Fourth Amendment protects the individual's privacy in a variety of settings. In none is the zone of privacy more clearly defined than when bounded by the unambiguous physical dimensions of an individual's home —a zone that finds its roots in clear and specific constitutional terms: "The right of the people to be secure in their . . . houses . . . shall not be violated." That language unequivocally establishes the proposition that "[a]t the very core of the Fourth Amendment stands the right of a man to retreat into his own home and there be free from unreasonable government intrusion." In terms that apply equally to seizures of property and to seizures of persons, the Fourth Amendment has drawn a firm line at the entrance of the house.

Given the very strong privacy right that is invaded when police search a home, the rule is clear that a police officer seeking to search a home must, with few exceptions, first obtain a search warrant.

A Home's Curtilage Also Gets Maximum Protection

IN addition to cloaking your home with a great deal of protection against the prying eyes of the government, the courts have developed the legal concept of a home's "curtilage." This concept was created to provide the same level of protection to the areas just outside a home which most people consider to be just as private as the interior of their home. The details of what is and isn't considered part of a home's curtilage are discussed in the next chapter because most curtilage issues involve Cannabis gardens. For now, you need only understand that all the rules in this chapter that apply to the home itself also apply to the home's curtilage.

Search Warrants

As discussed earlier, a search conducted under the authorization of a search warrant is presumed to be reasonable and hence legal. The method of obtaining a search warrant is relatively straightforward. A police officer simply writes out an affidavit explaining to a judge why he has probable cause to believe that a search of a particular place will turn up marijuana. If the judge is convinced by the officer's affidavit, the judge signs the search warrant and the officer runs off to prepare to conduct the search.

The purpose of requiring a search warrant is to take some power away from the police and vest it in a neutral judge. For example, in one case, Judge Green in California received information that his tenant was cultivating Cannabis on his property. The judge investigated and confirmed that 15 Cannabis plants were growing on his rental property. He took Polaroid pictures of the plants and immediately notified the police. The police officer who received the information, prepared an affidavit for a search warrant and brought it back to Judge Green, who quickly signed the search warrant authorizing the officer to search the Judge's rental premises and to seize the marijuana plants. A higher court held that the search warrant issued by Judge Green was invalid because the judge was anything but a "neutral and detached magistrate" as required by the Fourth Amendment.

Not only must the magistrate be neutral, but he must be the one who concludes that probable cause exists for the search. For that reason, a police officer's affidavit must not simply state conclusions. Rather, the officer must present facts that allow a *judge* to conclude that marijuana will be found in the place to be searched. Search warrants are often attacked by defense counsel for having invalid affidavits which state only the officer's conclusions rather than facts.

There is an immense amount of law governing search warrants. However, only a few points are relevant for what a person should do who some day hears a knock at the door and the bone chilling words, "Police officers, we have a search warrant."

If you or your home are the target of police officers with a search warrant, the following scenario will likely be played out. First, the officers will knock on your door and announce their identity as police officers; they will also announce their purpose, such as "narcotics" or simply "search warrant." Immediately upon entry they will run from room to room and bring all the occupants into one room. One officer will usually show the search warrant to the homeowner and then begin a thorough search of the premises.

There is not much you can do if an officer arrives at your home with a search warrant. Hopefully, your home will be free of marijuana. The best thing to do in such a situation is to take several deep breaths and try to remain calm. Do not admit anything. Ask to see the search warrant and simply check it to see if your correct address is listed. Occasionally, sloppy police work will result in an error on the face of the warrant. If you discover such an error, immediately bring it to the attention of the officer in charge, and demand that they immediately stop searching and leave your premises. You should also check to confirm that it has been signed by a judge. Again, if no signature appears, call it to the attention of one of the officers and demand that they stop searching and leave your home.

If It's Nighttime You're Probably Safe

UNDER the laws of most states, search warrants may be executed only during daylight hours. In these states, an officer may execute a search warrant at night only if the warrant contains a specific clause that authorizes a nighttime execution. Such clauses are rare. The general rule is that a judge can authorize a nighttime execution of a search warrant only if he is presented with facts that indicate a nighttime execution is required to prevent the removal or destruction of evidence. For example, in one case in Vermont, police arrested a man who was cultivating Cannabis on public property. There was sufficient evidence to establish probable cause that more evidence would be found in the man's home, and a judge issued a search warrant. The warrant was signed by the judge at 10:00 P.M. and authorized the search "at any time." The officers arrived at the man's empty home at 1:00 A.M., entered the home pursuant to the search warrant, and found additional incriminating evidence.

The man argued that it was illegal for the officers to execute the search warrant after nightfall. He cited Vermont law, which explicitly states, "the warrant shall be served between the hours of 6:00 A.M. and 10:00 P.M. unless the warrant directs that it may be served at any time." He noted that the Vermont courts had interpreted this law as justifying a nighttime search only where there is evidence that unless the search warrant was executed at night, there was a danger that the evidence sought would be destroyed or hidden. He argued that there was no danger of destruction of evidence because he was in jail at the time the search warrant was executed, and so could not possibly have destroyed evidence located at the home.

The Vermont Supreme Court rejected the man's argument. The court explained that although the man was in jail when the search warrant was obtained and executed, he was married. Therefore, in the court's words:

> The very real possibility existed that appellant's fate had become known or would become known before the night was over, and that this would prompt removal of the incriminating evidence by others. The judicial officer [who authorized the nighttime search] knew from the affidavits that [the appellant] had a wife. He could have reasonably concluded that the spouse might upon learning of her husband's apprehension seek to destroy any incriminating evidence and that an immediate search was warranted.

Consequently, the Vermont Supreme Court upheld the warrant's nighttime execution as well as the man's conviction for cultivating Cannabis.

The Knock-Notice Rule

EVEN with a warrant, a police officer may not enter a person's home without first knocking and announcing his presence. This is known as the "knock-notice rule." The rule requires that the officer knock on the door of the home to be searched, and give notice that he is a police officer. The officer must also give the occupants a reasonable amount of time to open the door. If no person answers, or the officer hears rustling inside that might indicate that the people are getting weapons or disposing of contraband, he may immediately enter the home by force.

In many states, when a warrant is issued to search a residence believed to contain marijuana or other drugs, courts will authorize the officers to execute the warrant without first knocking and giving notice of their search. These courts, however, require that the search warrant affidavit include some factual basis to believe that notice to the occupants would result in them destroying the marijuana, arming themselves, or escaping.

Warrants and the Plain-View Rule

IF police officers are legally searching a home pursuant to a warrant, they may seize any illegal items which they find while searching. However, the criminal nature of the items must be immediately apparent. For example, if a search warrant authorizes a search for marijuana and during that search the officers find some cocaine, they may seize the cocaine because it is clearly illegal. Likewise, if a search warrant authorizes a search for a gun, and the officers find marijuana while searching, they may legally seize the marijuana.

People on the Scene

WHAT about visitors who happen to be present when the police unexpectedly arrive with a search warrant? Can the police search them? In most situations the answer is "no." In most states the officers are restricted to searching only those persons or places specifically listed in the warrant. In most cases, a search warrant authorizes the search of only named individuals who reside at the residence to be searched. In such cases, the police can not search other people who just happen to be there when the police execute the search warrant. The police can detain and *frisk* all persons present, but only for the purpose of detecting weapons, not for the purpose of finding contraband. Of course, the police can also search any person who consents to a search.

Occasionally, the police will have information leading them to believe that a particular home is exclusively used for growing or "manufacturing" marijuana. In such cases, the courts of some states will permit the search warrant to contain a rather general authorization permitting the police to search "any or all persons on the premises."

There is one situation in which the police can search a visitor who is not named in the search warrant. If during a search pursuant to a warrant, an officer uncovers evidence establishing probable cause to believe that a visitor is concealing contraband, or involved in unlawful activity, then the officer can arrest that person and search him or her incident to arrest.

For example, in one case, Mary Lou was visiting her friends Bob and Larry at their fancy penthouse apartment. As they spoke, they were suddenly interrupted by a loud pounding at the door. Thinking it must be another friend, Bob yelled out, "Come in, it's open." At that moment the door flew open, and five police officers ran into the apartment. The officers yelled for them to get on the ground with their hands out to their sides.

Without believing what was happening, the three followed the officers' orders and hit the ground. The officers quickly ran through the apartment to check for other occupants. Another officer advised Larry and Bob that he had a search warrant for their apartment authorizing a search for marijuana and evidence of its sale. Because Bob and Larry were listed in the search warrant, the officers searched their pockets, finding a half-smoked joint and $350 on Bob. The officer took the joint and the money. The officers found nothing on Larry. Last, the officers pat-searched Mary Lou but felt no hard objects.

Inside Bob's bedroom, the officers found 13 vacuum-packed ounces of marijuana. Inside Larry's room, the officers found a professional quality scale, $950 in cash, and a well-used vacuum-packing machine. The officers confronted Bob and Larry with their discoveries, but the two men remained silent.

As the search warrant authorized, the officers checked the apartment for a telephone answering machine and found one in the kitchen. They played back the last message and heard a female voice leave the message, "Hey, you guys, it's Friday 3:00 P.M. If it's O.K., I'll drop by around 5:00 P.M. with the money. I really need the stuff for the weekend. See you later." The officers checked their watches, and realized it was 5:20 P.M. on Friday. Putting two and two together, the officers confronted Mary Lou, and asked her if she left a message. Mary Lou refused to answer. One of the officers then grabbed Mary Lou's jacket and searched inside its pockets. Inside the left pocket he found a vacuum-packed ounce of marijuana very similar to the 13 recovered in Bob's room. The officers then arrested Mary Lou, Bob, and Larry.

Mary Lou's attorney argued that the officer's search of Mary Lou's jacket was illegal, because she was not named in the search warrant, and did not even live at the apartment. The court rejected the argument. The court reasoned that the tape-recorded message in a female voice, the time correspondence between the message and Mary Lou's presence at the apartment, and the $350 found on Bob, all combined to give the officers probable cause to believe that Mary Lou had just purchased marijuana from the two men and was currently in possession of the marijuana. Therefore the court held that the officers' search of Mary Lou was legal, despite the fact that she was a visitor to the apartment and was not listed in the search warrant.

If It's Your Home, It's Presumed to Be Your Pot

A question that often arises when officers execute a search warrant and find several visitors at the home, as well as some marijuana, is whether the visitors can be convicted of possessing the marijuana merely because they were at the premises. As a general rule, any concealed marijuana found on premises which you control is presumed to be in your possession. You may be able to disprove or rebut that presumption if you can show facts which indicate you either were not aware of the drug's presence or had no control over it.

This rule makes sense because, as the owner or renter of a room, you have the most control over the items concealed in the room. Therefore, if the police find a resident and a nonresident in a room in which concealed marijuana is also found, the resident will be presumed to be the one in possession of the marijuana. The visitor can still be convicted of possessing the marijuana, but the prosecution must present evidence linking the visitor to the marijuana as well as establishing the other necessary elements of the crime of possession.

In one such case, the police entered a home pursuant to a search warrant and found a visitor and the homeowner in the bedroom. Underneath a chair on which the visitor was sitting, the officers found marijuana. The court held that in such circumstances there was *insufficient* evidence to convict the visitor of possession. The court stated:

> where a person is present in premises where marijuana is found, but does not have exclusive access, use or possession of the premises, it may not be inferred that he had knowledge of the presence of marijuana and had control of it unless there are additional independent factors showing his knowledge and control.

Most courts agree with the above quote, and require more than a visitor's mere presence to convict him or her of possessing concealed marijuana found on someone else's premises. A case from Texas gives a good example of the sort of additional evidence needed to convict a visitor in such a situation. In this case, police officers entered a home with a search warrant and found four people seated at a table playing cards. Approximately four feet from the table, the officers found a shoe box containing two bags of marijuana. In addition to the marijuana, the officers also found a letter addressed to one of the visiting card players. Although the player was a visitor to the residence, and although the marijuana was concealed from view, the court upheld the visitor's possession conviction on the reasoning that the letter linked him to the concealed marijuana.

One final note regarding visitors. If the police search a person's home and find marijuana concealed on the person of a visitor, the above rules work to protect the home owner. In other words, the home owner is *not* presumed to be the possessor of marijuana which is found concealed on the person of a visitor.

The Plain-View Rule and Your Home

THE plain-view rule can operate in several different fashions with regard to marijuana seen in plain view inside a person's home. If an officer is legally inside a person's home, any marijuana seen therein may be lawfully seized without a warrant. In fact, many arrests for marijuana result from police officers' inadvertently discovering evidence of marijuana use when they legally go to a home for some other reason. Obviously, in order not to become another one of those unlucky arrestees, one should strive to keep marijuana concealed, even in one's own home.

In contrast to the above rule, if an officer is *outside* a person's home, and from a lawful viewpoint observes through a person's window that there is Cannabis growing inside the home or its curtilage, the plain-view rule establishes only probable cause that Cannabis can be found inside the home. Yet, as explained earlier, probable cause is *insufficient* for an officer to conduct a warrantless entry of a home if he has neither exigent circumstances or consent. In other words, an officer's observation of marijuana in plain view does not entitle the officer to *enter* the home without a warrant. (In contrast, if an officer sees marijuana inside a car, while standing outside the car at a lawful viewpoint, the officer *is* legally entitled to conduct a warrantless search of the automobile. Why? Because the automobile is considered less private than a person's home, and hence, as discussed in Chapter 5, probable cause *is* sufficient for an officer to search a vehicle without a warrant.)

Consenting to a Search of Your Home

How is it that, if most searches do not occur with search warrants, police find so much marijuana in people's homes? Well, the sad fact is that people, usually without thinking, invite the police into their homes. Simply stated, and as explained earlier, voluntary consent to a search automatically makes the search legal. The courts reason that if you allow the police to come into your home and conduct a warrantless search, then you cannot later turn around and argue that the warrantless search was illegal. Moreover, unintentional consent is considered valid consent. For example, in one case, a police officer knocked on the door of a suspected marijuana user. From inside came the response, "Yeah, come in." The officer walked in and immediately saw a Cannabis plant on the kitchen floor. The court held that the homeowner's consent was valid, even though he was unaware that it was a police officer who sought entry. The court noted that the officer did not make any fraudulent statements nor was the occupant under any duress when he consented to the entry. Therefore the occupant's consent was voluntarily given, even though he did not know that it was a police officer who sought entry.

Occasionally a police officer, suspecting a person of marijuana use, will go to the person's home in hopes of tricking the person into consenting to the officer's entry into and/or search of the home. Most courts have held that when an officer uses a trick to get the occupant to consent to a warrantless entry or search, the consent is invalid; hence the subsequent entry and search are illegal. Therefore any evidence found after such warrantless entry should be excluded.

For example, the courts have routinely held that it is illegal for police officers to gain entry to a home by falsely telling the occupant that they have a search warrant or arrest warrant. Another trick that one court has found to negate the homeowner's consent is explained in the Illinois case of Richard Daugherty.

In this case, Richard Daugherty reported to the police that some money was missing from his home. A police officer was dispatched to the Daugherty household and made a report of the apparent theft. A few days later, the parents of the Daugherty's babysitter called Mr. Daugherty to report that their daughter had taken the money one night while baby-sitting. The police were notified of this information and questioned the babysitter regarding the theft. During the questioning, the babysitter volunteered that she had seen evidence of marijuana use while baby-sitting at the Daugherty home.

Officer Barts of the local police department was given this information, and set out to try to arrest Richard Daugherty for possession of marijuana. However, Officer Barts did not get a search warrant. Rather, several days after taking the information from the babysitter, Officer Barts arrived unannounced at the Daugherty household, and asked for permission to come in, "to conduct further inspection regarding the theft." Daugherty's wife, Karen, consented to the officer's entry for such purpose. Once Barts was inside the home, he began asking Karen questions about the theft that were designed to get her to show him around the home.

For example, the officer asked her to show him from where the money was taken. Next, he asked her to show him where else in the home the Daugherty's kept money. Officer Barts' hope was that he would spot evidence of marijuana use while Karen took him from room to room showing him where they kept their money. Just as the officer had hoped, when Karen took him into the kitchen, Barts saw some marijuana in plain view on the kitchen countertop. He seized the marijuana, arrested Karen and Robert Daugherty, and called for backup. Under the pressure of the situation, the Daughertys confessed that more marijuana could be found in several places in the home. Robert Daugherty also turned over a scale and several pipes used to smoke marijuana.

Fortunately, the Daugherty's lawyer heard what happened and how Officer Barts tricked Karen into consenting to the officer's entry. The lawyer argued that the officer's warrantless entry was illegal, because Karen's consent was procured through a trick by Officer Barts. The Illinois Court of Appeal found that Barts went to the Daugherty's residence to gain entry and search for evidence of marijuana use, and that the theft investigation was a subterfuge to trick Karen into consenting to his entry of the home. Therefore the court agreed with the Daugherty's attorney and ordered that Robert Daugherty's conviction for possession of marijuana be reversed. (The charges against Karen had already been dropped.) The court explained that when a person gives consent to a police officer's warrantless entry of their home, the consent must be *voluntarily* given. The court reasoned:

> Where, as here, the law-enforcement officer without a warrant uses his official position of authority and falsely claims that he has legitimate police business to conduct in order to gain consent to enter the premises when, in fact, his real reason is to search inside for evidence of a crime, we find that this deception under the circumstances is so unfair as to be coercive and renders the consent invalid. This police conduct offends the Fourth Amendment and is fundamentally unfair when compared with the need for effective police investigation.

Who Can Consent to a Search of Your House or Apartment?

OFTEN the issue arises as to whether someone else can consent to the search of your home. For example, can your landlord or roommate consent to the search of your apartment? To a large extent, the answer depends on what relationship the person giving consent has to the home that the police wish to search.

Landlords

LANDLORDS have no authority to consent to the search of your apartment, so long as you are legally entitled to possess the premises. In other words, if you have paid your rent or are not in the process of being evicted, your landlord has no authority to consent to an officer's request to search your apartment. Any consent your landlord might give will be considered ineffective by a court; so anything an officer finds during such a search should not be used to convict you. The rule with respect to landlords also applies to hotel owners and hotel employees. In other words, a hotel clerk, janitor, or maid has no authority to consent to an officer's request to search your hotel room.

Roommates

FOR roommates the answer is slightly more complicated. If your roommate is home alone when the police arrive, he can consent to a search of any area that he shares with you. Courts have held that you maintain no reasonable expectation of privacy in such common areas, because your roommate has a right to invite his friends or guests into them. However, your roommate cannot consent to a search of any areas that you alone inhabit. For instance, if you have a separate private bedroom, then your roommate may not consent to a search of that room.

Suppose both you and your roommate are home when the police arrive. Can your roommate consent to a search of the common areas over your objection? Under a Supreme Court decision, the answer seems to be that your objection is irrelevant. The police may search the common areas based on the consent of your roommate alone. Accordingly, you should be aware that when you decide to have a roommate, you are potentially giving up a portion of your Fourth Amendment privacy rights, at least in the common living areas. The same rule applies to your spouse and anyone else you allow to live with you.

In contrast, most courts hold that your roommate or spouse may not consent over your objection if he or she is away from the apartment. For example, in one case, the police lawfully arrested Charles for possession of marijuana after stopping him for a traffic violation. Charles denied that he possessed any other marijuana and gave the police his key to the apartment, so that they could search it to confirm that he possessed no other marijuana.

When the officers arrived at the apartment, Charles' roommate, Roger, was home and refused to allow the police to enter. The officers, disregarding his objection, forcibly entered the apartment, found marijuana inside, and charged Roger with possession. The court that heard the case held that the officers search of the apartment was illegal! Therefore the case against Roger was dismissed for lack of evidence. This case created the rule that a roommate who is away from the premises may not authorize police to enter and search the premises if the other roommate is in the premises and objects to the police entry and searching.

Children

CAN your child consent to a search of your home? The answer to this question depends on the age of the child. In one case, the consent of an 11-year-old child was held to be ineffective on the theory that a child cannot waive the privacy rights of his or her parents. However, the older the child, the greater the chances that a court will find the child's consent valid. In addition, consent by a child has been found valid when the child was the victim or witness of a crime, and was admitting the police for that reason.

Your Home and "Exigent Circumstances"

As was mentioned earlier, an officer can legally search a person's home without a warrant if "exigent circumstances" exist. The California Supreme Court has defined the exigent circumstances sufficient to justify a warrantless search of a home as follows:

> [E]xigent circumstances means an emergency situation requiring swift action to prevent imminent danger to life or serious damage to property, or to forestall the imminent escape of a suspect or destruction of evidence.

In one case, Mr. Robinson was at home when undercover police officers came to his home to try to purchase marijuana. Mr. Robinson evidently had some suspicions and refused to let the officers inside. However, when he partially opened the door to tell them to go away, one officer saw a large bag containing marijuana just inside the door. The officer blocked the door with his foot, thereby allowing the other officers to push their way into Mr. Robinson's home and arrest him. The court upheld the officer's warrantless arrest of Mr. Robinson on the grounds that immediate action was necessary to prevent the destruction of the evidence.

Obviously, anyone having Cannabis plants or marijuana in his home, should be more careful than usual about admitting people into his home. If possible, you should install a "peephole" in your door to permit you to distinguish friend from foe without even opening your door or revealing your presence. If you do not have a peephole, you should respond to any unexpected knocks just like mother taught you—simply ask, "Who is it?" Do not open the door unless you are absolutely sure it is someone you know and trust.

If the day comes when the response to your question is, "Police officers," you may legally keep your door *shut* and ask them (through the door) what they want. You do not have to open your door unless they tell you they have a warrant. In one case, officers received a call that the occupants of a specific residence were using narcotics. The officers went to the house and knocked on the door. When someone inside opened the door, the officers were engulfed in the "odor of burning marijuana emanating from within." The court held that the officers acted legally in immediately entering the home without a warrant, because any delay might have resulted in the destruction of the marijuana. Therefore the officer's warrantless entry was justified by exigent circumstances.

Another way exigent circumstances can arise is when someone commits a serious crime and is being chased by police officers. If the suspect is seen to enter a home, the police do not have to get an arrest warrant authorizing them to enter and arrest the suspect. The courts have held that such situations require the officers to act without delay. Therefore the exigent-circumstances rule permits the officers to kick the door down and arrest the suspect without first obtaining a warrant.

In the same vein, if officers reasonably believe that it is necessary to act immediately to save someone's life or to prevent serious bodily injury, they may enter a home without first obtaining a warrant. For example, John and Cindy were both unemployed and lived in a one-room apartment in a high-crime area. To support themselves, John and Cindy cultivated a yearly crop of approximately 40 Cannabis plants. To relieve their stress, John and Cindy engaged in weekly primal scream sessions.

One Friday evening, after John had checked the pH level of all his plants, he let loose with several blood curdling high intensity screams to purge himself of the week's accumulated stress. John allowed himself to collapse on the couch, enjoying a feeling of total relaxation.

Suddenly, John heard a loud knock at his door, followed by the announcement, "Police officers! Open the door!" Frozen in fear, John sat there, not knowing how to react. Fifteen seconds after the knock, John's front door was kicked in, and two police officers ran into his apartment with their guns drawn. Immediately upon entering, the cops saw the Cannabis plants and quickly placed John under arrest.

The officers' entry of John's home was legal under the exigent-circumstances rule. The police officers, hearing John's scream, reasonably believed that someone in John's apartment was in need of emergency assistance or possibly the victim of a brutal crime. Therefore the officers' warrantless entry was legal under the exigent-circumstances exception to the warrant requirement. Accordingly, the plants were properly introduced in court, and John was convicted of Cannabis cultivation.

In contrast to the above example, if a court finds that a police officer did not have a good reason to think that a warrantless entry was immediately required, the court should find the officer's warrantless entry illegal and exclude any evidence he found. For example, in one case:

> Officer Del Rosso testified that about 9:40 P.M , on September 26, 1979, accompanied by a factory custodian, he was searching the third floor of a factory for intruders. The factory was about 40' distant (across a 32' street) from the "three-decker" apartment house in which, on the third floor, Huffman lived as a tenant. The officer's attention was attracted by lighted windows without curtains or shades. Through the windows (before he called for assistance) he observed for an appreciable time, Huffman and two other men taking a green herb from one bag and putting it into numerous other smaller bags. Officer Del Rosso called for police assistance and then obtained binoculars . . . from his police cruiser. He was joined by several other officers. With them, he observed Huffman and the other men through two different windows for about fifteen minutes more.

The officers went to the apartment house, found "the first door downstairs" open and the hall door unlocked. They proceeded to the third floor landing. Huffman's apartment door was partially ajar (about five or six inches), music was "blaring," and there was a strong odor [of] marijuana. Through the open door, he observed one of the men "still bagging" the green herb. The officers entered and found the three men, previously observed from the factory, sitting or standing near a table two or three feet from the windows. On a table were sixteen "baggies" containing the green herb and fifteen hand-rolled cigarettes strewn around the table. The herb on analysis proved to be marijuana. No attempt was made to obtain a search or arrest warrant. Officer Del Rosso's cruiser and the other officers' cruisers were parked in an alley out of sight of the apartment building."

The Supreme Court of Massachusetts held that the officers' warrantless entry of Michael Huffman's apartment was illegal because the prosecutor failed to prove that exigent circumstances existed. First, nothing indicated that Michael or his friends were armed or that they might attempt to escape. In fact, nothing indicated that Michael or his friends were even aware of the officer's presence. Therefore, the officers had no reason to believe that immediate action was necessary to prevent Michael from destroying the marijuana. As a result, the court reversed Michael's conviction for possessing marijuana with the intent to distribute.

Officers Who "Threaten" to Get a Search Warrant

GIVEN the above examples, it should be clear that anyone desiring to speak with police officers who unexpectedly come to his home without a warrant, would be wise to do so without opening the door. At the very least, such conversations should be conducted outside of the home rather than inviting the officers inside.

It is possible that some day a police officer will come to your home without a search warrant and accuse you of some sort of marijuana crime. The officer will tell you that he wants to search your home for marijuana, and that you should have nothing to worry about if you are innocent. He will also tell you that if you do not consent to a search, he will get a search warrant. He will tell you to make it easy on yourself and just consent.

You should never consent under these conditions. This tactic is almost always used when an officer knows that he does not have enough evidence to get a search warrant. (Obviously, if the officer really did have sufficient evidence against you, he would have obtained a search warrant already.) Therefore you may legally refuse to allow the search in the absence of a search warrant. Once the officer leaves, many wise people consider eliminating all evidence of marijuana for at least the next two weeks. However, they are careful when doing such a cleanup. In one case, an officer parked outside a person's home, waiting for him to come running out with a large amount of marijuana in his hands!

7. Gardens

You may be interested to learn that, at least in the eyes of the legal system, all Cannabis gardens are not created equal. Rather, the United States Supreme Court has held that some gardens deserve more protection than others. Specifically, the constitutional protections afforded a person's Cannabis garden depend on whether the garden is located: (1) inside a home; or (2) outside a home, but inside the home's curtilage; or (3) outside a home, and outside the home's curtilage.

Those gardens located inside a home have the greatest constitutional protection against searches by police officers. Those gardens located outside a home, but within a home's curtilage, while in theory entitled to the same protection as those inside a home, in practice receive less protection. Lastly, a garden located outside a home, and outside the home's curtilage, receives very little, if any, protection.

Cannabis Gardens in the Home

As noted above, a Cannabis garden located inside the four walls and under the roof of a home is entitled to the same stringent constitutional protections as every other item located in the home. Therefore the law concerning such gardens is explained in Chapter 6.

Cannabis Gardens inside the Curtilage of a Home

As mentioned in Chapter 6, the United States Supreme Court has interpreted the federal constitution as providing maximum protection against a police officer's search not only of a home, but also of what it has termed the "curtilage" of a home. Roughly speaking, a home's curtilage is that area that closely surrounds the outside of the home and in which the average resident expects a high degree of privacy.

The United States Supreme Court has formulated a test for deciding what is, and what is not, included in a home's curtilage. Under this test, the

Court examines "whether the area harbors the intimate activity associated with the sanctity of a man's home and the privacies of life." If a court concludes that an area is within the curtilage of a home, the police must have a search warrant (or an exception to the warrant requirement) in order to search the area.

It is clear from numerous cases that a home's curtilage is limited to the area very near the home itself. The Supreme Court has refused to create a "bright-line rule," which would classify an area as "curtilage" if it was within a set distance from the home. Rather, the court has spelled out four important factors that help to define a home's curtilage. The factors are:

1. The proximity of the area to the home.
2. Whether the area is included within an enclosure surrounding the home.
3. The nature of the uses to which the area is put.
4. The steps taken by the resident to protect the area from observation by people passing by.

An example of how the Court applies these factors when ruling on a police officer's warrantless search is given by the case of Mr. Dunn. In this case, DEA agents received information that Mr. Dunn had a large quantity of chemicals used to manufacture illegal drugs delivered to his ranch in a truck. The agents took aerial photographs of Mr. Dunn's ranch and found that the truck was parked outside a barn located approximately sixty yards from his home. The agents also discovered from the photographs that Mr. Dunn's ranch was quite a fortress. The photos revealed that Dunn's ranch was completely encircled by a perimeter fence. In addition, there were several interior barbed-wire fences, one of which encircled the home, but did not encircle the barn. The front of the barn was blocked by an additional wooden fence with locked waist-high gates.

One evening, disregarding every fence encountered along their path, several DEA agents snuck up to Dunn's barn to investigate whether he was manufacturing drugs. They could hear a motor running in the barn and could smell a chemical associated with illicit drug manufacturing. Based on these observations, the agents obtained a search warrant for the barn that led to the seizure of drug-manufacturing equipment and chemicals, as well as to the arrest of Mr. Dunn.

Mr. Dunn argued that the agents' initial search, which brought them onto his property and up to the barn, was illegal because they invaded the curtilage of his home without a warrant. The United States Supreme Court rejected Dunn's argument, finding the barn was not inside the curtilage of

Dunn's home. The Court explained that the barn was a substantial distance from the home (60 yards), and was not treated as an adjunct of the home. Second, the barn was not within the fence that surrounded the home and that marked off the area that is part and parcel of the home. Third, the agents had information prior to their entry that the barn was not used as part of the home, but rather as an exterior drug lab. Last, the Court explained that Dunn did little to protect the barn from observation by people standing outside the property. The Court noted that the fences were all of the see-through variety, of the type used to corral livestock, rather than the type of solid tall fence that is used to ensure privacy. Therefore, the Court concluded, the agents never entered the curtilage of Dunn's home and hence no warrant was required.

Creating a Curtilage in the Eyes of a Court

ANYONE desiring the increased privacy protection given to a home's curtilage would be wise to implement the four factors discussed above. For example, a gardener desiring maximum constitutional protection for his garden would want to situate his garden within the curtilage, by placing it as close to the home as possible and by making it very clear that he reasonably expects privacy in the area.

If a court finds that a person's garden was within the curtilage of his home, the court will be forced to give the garden increased protection under the constitution. This means that police cannot legally enter the garden without first obtaining a warrant, or without acting under one of the exceptions to the warrant requirement. For example, in one case, a sheriff observed Cannabis plants growing in plain view next to a man's home. The area, although not fenced off, was clearly within the curtilage of the man's home. Without getting a warrant, the sheriff walked up to the plants and pulled them up. The man was subsequently convicted of cultivating marijuana.

On appeal, the sheriff's warrantless seizure of the plants was declared illegal. The appellate court explained that the sheriff's plain-view *observation* of the Cannabis plants was entirely legal and gave the sheriff probable cause. However, because the plants were within the curtilage of the man's home, the sheriff's act of *physically entering* the curtilage without first obtaining a warrant was illegal under the Constitution. Therefore, the court of appeal reversed the man's conviction, holding that the illegally seized plants should have been excluded from evidence.

Increasing the privacy of a garden is a matter of common sense.

Anything that separates a garden from the mass of humanity is a plus. This includes fences and walls around the garden, and making use of all natural boundaries such as mountains, hedges, trees, and streams. Posting "No Trespassing" signs around the perimeter of the garden is wise.

In one case, a police officer peered through a knothole in a wooden fence and saw what he believed were Cannabis plants growing in Patrick Lovelace's backyard. He used his observations as the basis for a search warrant of the residence. In court, Patrick argued that the officer's first view of his garden was an illegal search, because the officer unreasonably invaded the privacy of his curtilage by peeking through the knothole. Patrick's attorney was able to get the officer to admit in court that he could not see over or under the fence, and was able to gain his view of the garden only by peering through a one-inch-wide knothole. The officer also testified that there were very few holes in the fence. To counter Patrick's arguments, the prosecutor argued that the marijuana was in plain view because the officer was on a public sidewalk, and anyone could have looked through the knothole.

The court agreed with Patrick, and found the officer's search unlawful. The court based its decision on the fact that the officer originally viewed the plants by placing his face within one inch of the fence. Therefore, although the officer was legally on public property when he looked through the knothole, the judge deemed the officer's action unreasonable and illegal, because there was no evidence that pedestrians ordinarily got within one inch of the knothole to spy into Patrick's backyard.

The cases make clear that a person must protect his garden not only from people who may pass by at ground level, but also from possible viewing from aboveground. In many cases, a person's failure to protect his garden from the prying eyes of his neighbor's second-storey window has proven fatal. For example, in one case, police officers were able to identify 77 Cannabis plants in the curtilage of a woman's backyard by viewing the plants from a neighbor's second-storey window. The court held that although the garden was inside the curtilage of the gardener's home and could not have been viewed in any other manner, the gardener had no reasonable expectation of privacy, given that the plants could be seen in plain view from her neighbor's window.

Likewise, the United States Supreme Court has held that under certain circumstances a police officer's aerial surveillance of a person's Cannabis plants, even if within the curtilage of a home, violates no reasonable expectation of privacy and hence is not a "search" within the meaning of the Fourth Amendment.

Cannabis Gardens Situated Outside a Home's Curtilage

THE United States Supreme Court has held that any land outside of a home's curtilage maintains no reasonable expectation of privacy, despite an owner's attempt to keep the public out! This remarkable rule is known as the doctrine of "open fields." The Supreme Court has defined an open field as "any unoccupied or undeveloped area outside the curtilage. An open field need be neither 'open' nor a 'field' as those terms are used in common speech." The Supreme Court first applied the "open fields" doctrine to a marijuana case in 1984, when it examined a police officer's search of land owned by Ray Oliver.

In this case, the Supreme Court held that Ray Oliver maintained *no* legitimate expectation of privacy in his Cannabis garden, despite the fact that the garden was located on Mr. Oliver's property in a highly secluded area, bounded on all sides by woods, fences, and embankments, which prevented its observation from any point of public access. Additionally, Mr. Oliver had posted "No Trespassing" signs around the perimeter of his property.

Similarly, in a case decided that same day, the Supreme Court held that Richard Thornton had no reasonable expectation of privacy in his Cannabis garden located in a secluded wooded area on his property, surrounded by a chicken-wire fence and posted with "No Trespassing" signs!

The court reached its astounding decision by reading the Constitution extremely narrowly and finding that the Fourth Amendment's protection for "persons, houses, papers, and effects" does not extend to areas beyond the immediate surrounding of a home. In the Court's words, "an individual may not legitimately demand privacy for activities conducted out of doors in fields, except in the area immediately surrounding the home." The Court explained that the term "open fields" is not to be interpreted literally but rather includes "any unoccupied or undeveloped area outside of the curtilage." Therefore, even thickly wooded areas such as those hiding Mr. Oliver's and Mr. Thornton's gardens can be considered "open fields" and hence entirely unprotected by the Fourth Amendment.

In this remarkable opinion, the Supreme Court stated that it is *impossible* for an individual to establish a legitimate expectation of privacy in an area of land outside of a home's curtilage. The Court stated:

> We reject the suggestion that steps taken to protect privacy
> established that expectations of privacy in an open field are

legitimate. It is true, of course, that [Mr.] Oliver and [Mr.] Thornton, in order to conceal their criminal activities, planted the marijuana upon secluded land and erected fences and "No Trespassing" signs around the property. And it may be that because of such precautions, few members of the public stumbled upon the marijuana crops seized by the police. Neither of these suppositions demonstrates, however, that the expectation of privacy was legitimate in the sense required by the Fourth Amendment. The test of legitimacy is not whether the individual chooses to conceal assertively "private" activity. Rather, the correct inquiry is whether the government's intrusion infringes upon the personal and societal values protected by the Fourth Amendment. As we have explained, we find no basis for concluding that a police inspection of open fields accomplishes such an infringement.

In reaching its decision, the Supreme Court agreed that the officers trespassed upon Mr. Oliver's and Mr. Thornton's property in order to locate the Cannabis gardens. Even so, the Court held that no warrant was needed because no Fourth Amendment protections applied. In the words of one court, "the Fourth Amendment prohibits unreasonable searches and seizures, not trespasses."

Searching Your Home Based on Seeing Your Garden

GENERALLY speaking, if police officers discover that a person is growing Cannabis in his backyard, the officers can use that information for a search warrant that authorizes them to search not only the person's backyard, but also the inside of the person's home. An actual affidavit in one such case stated:

From the public alleyway between Deluxe Cleaners and the residence at 116 Maynell, I was able to observe the backyard of 116 Maynell . . . . I noted at the southwest corner of a garage and next to the fence and alleyway, several marijuana plants numbering at least four, ranging from three- to five-feet tall. These plants appear to have been well cared for and appear to have been specifically planted in that location as there are no other marijuana plants within the backyard. I noted that the ground around the base of the plants was moist, with the plants appearing to have been watered. I noted that these marijuana plants had the characteristics of the marijuana plant in its growing state, being medium to dark green in color and having sawtoothed-edge leaves. Being an expert on the identification of growing marijuana plants, it is my opinion that the plants observed by your affiant were, in fact, marijuana plants in their growing state.

As an experienced narcotics officer I can also say that in the past on numerous occasions regarding the cultivation of marijuana . . . I have found amounts of marijuana plants inside of a residence and outbuildings on the property being cured and manicured for the use and sale of these plants. I can further say that marijuana grown by private individuals is picked and commonly taken into residences and outbuildings to be dried and manicured. I have further found that individuals involved in the cultivation of marijuana plants keep inside of their residence and outbuildings marijuana seeds. As an expert on the identification of marijuana I can also state that marijuana is usually hung and dried out of view of the public. Marijuana is also frequently manicured and packaged for use and sale and this requires all types of implements and is also generally done out of view of the public. For those reasons I believe that there can be found inside of the residence at 116 Maynell, Modesto, California, marijuana and the implements used to cultivate and package marijuana for use or sale.

Presented with such an affidavit, almost every judge will find that a backyard Cannabis garden establishes probable cause that marijuana will be found inside the home. Consequently, such a search warrant can legally permit the officers to search the inside of the grower's home. However, at least one court in California has held that an officer's observation of a *single* Cannabis plant in a person's backyard may not establish probable cause that marijuana will be found inside the person's home.

In this case, Officer Miller of the San Diego Police Department received information that Mitchell Pellegrin was cultivating Cannabis in his backyard. The officer investigated and saw in plain view a single "three-foot marijuana plant growing next to a fence at the rear of Pellegrin's residence." Based on his observations, Officer Miller obtained a search warrant and searched Pellegrin's home. Inside, he found some concentrated Cannabis.

The court held that the search warrant was invalid because Officer Miller's observation of a single marijuana plant in Pellegrin's backyard was insufficient to establish probable cause that marijuana could be found in Pellegrin's house. Why? Because, as the court pointed out, the single plant could have been growing wild without Pellegrin's knowledge. Officer Miller failed to state in his affidavit any facts indicating that the plant was being "cultivated." The court ended its opinion by stating, "the right of the people of the United States of America to be secure in the privacy of their homes is upon too solid a foundation to be undermined by what could well be a happenstance growing of one marijuana plant in a yard."

In contrast, courts have held that a handful of Cannabis plants observed growing in pots in a person's backyard *does* establish probable cause that additional evidence of marijuana use or cultivation will be found inside the residence. As one court stated, "marijuana plants do not grow in pots and planters by chance. When they are found growing in that manner, it is reasonable to infer those who controlled and occupied the premises have something to do with their planting, cultivation, or care."

Police Fly-overs

AERIAL surveillance by the police is becoming an increasingly common search method. For example, in recent years in California, the state has implemented a "Campaign Against Marijuana Planting," known as CAMP for short. CAMP's mode of operation is to use airplanes and helicopters to locate Cannabis gardens. In fact, CAMP has even used high-altitude U2 planes for detection and surveillance of marijuana crops! (A federal court approved of the use of the U2 planes, but expressed its distaste for such domestic use of spy planes.) In its first two years of operation, CAMP seized hundreds of thousands of pounds of Cannabis plants, valued at hundreds of millions of dollars.

Currently, FAA regulations permit fixed-wing aircraft to be flown as low as 1,000 feet while over congested areas, and as low as 500 feet over uncongested areas. For helicopters, these regulations are even more lenient. The regulations permit helicopters to fly below the above altitudes, if the operation is conducted without hazard to person or property on the surface. Therefore, for helicopters, there is no set minimum altitude. However, in one case, a gardener was arrested for cultivating two Cannabis plants after a police officer in a helicopter identified the plants by hovering only 25 feet above them! The court was outraged by the officer's action, and promptly declared the search illegal.

In another case, Sheriff Jones in Florida received an anonymous tip that Riley was growing Cannabis on his property. Jones drove by Riley's home and found it to be a mobile home on five acres of rural property. Jones could see a greenhouse about fifteen feet behind the mobile home, but was unable to tell what, if anything, was growing inside it. He could see no Cannabis plants in open view.

Jones was not so easily convinced. He boarded a helicopter and flew over Riley's property. When he passed over the greenhouse, which was indisputably within the curtilage of Riley's home, the officer observed that it was covered with corrugated roofing panels, approximately 10 percent of which were missing. Jones ordered the helicopter pilot to descend to approximately 400 feet above the greenhouse. As he hovered above the gaps in the greenhouse roof, he looked through the openings with his naked eye and saw some Cannabis plants. Jones quickly returned to the station and wrote out an affidavit of probable cause to obtain a search warrant. A judge signed the warrant and Riley's greenhouse was searched, resulting in the seizure of some Cannabis plants, and the arrest of Riley.

Riley argued, all the way to the United States Supreme Court, that officer Jones's fly-over was an illegal warrantless search of his greenhouse, which was located within the curtilage of his home, and that the subsequent warrant was therefore invalid as being based on illegally obtained information.

The case split the Supreme Court. The five most conservative justices rejected Riley's argument, concluding that Sheriff Jones's view from the helicopter was not an unconstitutional search. However, they disagreed as to *why* the aerial view was legal under the constitution.

Four of these justices held that the aerial view was not a "search." In their opinion (termed the "plurality opinion"), the fact that the fly-over was permissible under the above-discussed FAA regulations, was sufficient to make it constitutional. In their words:

> Riley no doubt intended and expected that his greenhouse
> would not be open to public inspection, and the precautions
> he took protected against ground-level observation. Because
> the sides and roof of his greenhouse were left partially open,
> however, what was growing in the greenhouse was subject to
> viewing from the air . . . Any member of the public could

legally have been flying over Riley's property in a helicopter at the altitude of 400 feet and could have observed Riley's greenhouse. The police officer did no more.

They compared Riley's case to an earlier case where police officers spotted a person's Cannabis garden while flying at 1,000 feet. In that case, the Supreme Court held that the fly-over was constitutional, stating:

> In an age where private and commercial flight in the public airways is routine, it is unreasonable for respondent to expect that his marijuana plants were constitutionally protected from being observed with the naked eye from an altitude of 1,000 feet. The Fourth Amendment simply does not require the police traveling in the public airways at this altitude to obtain a warrant in order to observe what is visible to the naked eye.

The fifth conservative justice, Justice O'Connor, agreed that Jones's aerial surveillance was constitutional, but expressed concern that her conservative brethren placed undue reliance on FAA regulations. In her opinion, "[t]he fact that a helicopter could conceivably observe the curtilage at virtually any altitude or angle, without violating FAA regulations, does not in itself mean that an individual has no reasonable expectation of privacy from such observation." In short, in her opinion, the determinative factor in fly-over cases was whether or not public aircraft generally traveled at such altitudes. If such air traffic was relatively common, then a gardener surveilled by a police fly-over could not be said to have a reasonable expectation of privacy in his garden. Therefore, under such circumstances, an officer's aerial observation would be a constitutional plain-view observation. However, if low-level public fly-overs were very uncommon in the garden's location, then the gardener's expectation of privacy was more likely reasonable. Under those circumstances, an officer's fly-over, even if within FAA guidelines, would be an unconstitutional violation of the gardener's reasonable expectation of privacy. Having set forth her reasoning, Justice O'Connor then found that Riley failed to present any evidence that public fly-overs above his greenhouse were rare. Having no evidence that public fly-overs were uncommon, Justice O'Connor concurred with the plurality that Sheriff Jones's aerial surveillance did not offend Riley's reasonable expectation of privacy, and hence did not violate the Fourth Amendment.

Justice Brennan, along with three other justices, dissented. In the opinion of these justices, the plurality forsook the traditional "reasonable expectation of privacy" analysis in favor of total deference to FAA regulations. The dissenting justices agreed with Justice O'Connor that simply because an airborne police officer is in a place where he has a legal right to be (i.e., flying within FAA regulations), does not necessarily follow that whatever he sees from that vantage point was knowingly exposed to public view. In Brennan's opinion, the conservative justices who wrote the plurality opinion, were sacrificing the Fourth Amendment protections that safeguard the privacy rights of all citizens in order to facilitate fighting the war on drugs. Justice Brennan wrote:

> It is difficult to avoid the conclusion that the plurality has allowed its analysis of Riley's expectation of privacy to be colored by its distaste for the activity in which he was engaged. It is indeed easy to forget, especially in view of current concern over drug trafficking, that the scope of the Fourth Amendment's protection does not turn on whether the activity disclosed by a search is illegal or innocuous. But we dismiss this as a "drug case" only at the peril of our own liberties . . . .

> If the Constitution does not protect Riley's marijuana garden against such surveillance, it is hard to see how it will forbid the Government from aerial spying on the activities of a law-abiding citizen on her fully enclosed outdoor patio . . . .

> The issue in this case is, ultimately, "how tightly the Fourth Amendment permits people to be driven back into the recesses of their lives by the risk of surveillance." The Court today approves warrantless helicopter searches from an altitude of 400 feet. . . . I find considerable cause for concern in the fact that a plurality of four justices would remove virtually all constitutional barriers to police surveillance from the vantage point of helicopters. The Fourth Amendment demands that we temper our efforts to apprehend criminals with a concern for the impact on our fundamental liberties of the methods we use. I hope it will be a matter of concern to my colleagues that the police-surveillance methods they would sanction were among those described forty years ago in George Orwell's dread vision of life in the 1980s:

> > "The black-mustachio'd face gazed down from every commanding corner. There was one on the house-front immediately oppo-

site. BIG BROTHER IS WATCHING
YOU, the caption said . . . In the far distance a helicopter skimmed down between
roofs, hovered for an instant like a blue-
bottle, and darted away again with a curv-
ing flight. It was the Police Patrol, snoop-
ing into people's windows." G. Orwell,
Nineteen Eighty-Four (1949).

Who can read this passage without a shudder, and without
the instinctive reaction that it depicts life in some country
other than ours? I respectfully dissent.

So, after all of the above is said, what's the law with respect to aerial
surveillance by law enforcement? Currently, the rule is expressed by the *reasoning* of Justice O'Connor and the dissenting justices. While FAA guidelines
are an important factor, the federal constitutionality of a police officer's fly-
over is determined by looking at whether *public aircraft* commonly fly at such
altitudes *at the particular location surveilled.* In other words, if for one reason
or another, a person's garden is routinely exposed to the view of passing public
aircraft, a police officer's view from the same flight path does not violate the
gardener's reasonable expectation of privacy, and is therefore fully constitutional.
In contrast, if a person's garden is located in an area that very rarely or never
has public aircraft flying overhead a police officer's aerial surveillance of the
garden, even if within FAA regulations, violates the gardener's reasonable
expectation of privacy, and is therefore unconstitutional without a warrant.

It is worth stressing that this rule is currently in jeopardy because two
of the four dissenting justices who agreed with O'Connor' reasoning are no
longer on the Court and have been replaced by more conservative justices.
Therefore, when the next fly-over case comes before the Court, it is quite
likely that a majority of the justices will follow the plurality opinion in the
Riley case and hold that a police officer's fly-over is constitutional so long as it
was conducted in compliance with FAA regulations.

Currently, the supreme court of at least one state (California) has held
that although the United States Constitution may not provide much protection
against aerial observations of a person's curtilage, the *state* constitution *does*.

In a well-reasoned opinion, the California Supreme Court explained:

We were not persuaded that police officers who examine a
residence from the air are simply observing what is in "plain

view" from a lawful public vantage point. Such reasoning ignores the essential difference between ground and aerial surveillance. One can take reasonable steps to ensure his yard's privacy from the street, sidewalk, or neighborhood, and police on the ground may not broach such barriers to gain a view of the enclosed area. But there is no practical defense against aerial spying, and precious constitutional privacy rights would mean little if the government could defeat them so easily.

Even if members of the public may casually see into his yard when a routine flight happens over the property, we concluded, a householder does not thereby consent to focused examination of the curtilage by airborne police officers looking for evidence of crime. No law-enforcement interest justifies such intensive warrantless government intrusion into a zone of heightened constitutional privacy.

Unfortunately, California is rather unique, in that it has a rule that only evidence obtained in violation of the *federal* constitution is excluded. Therefore, despite the California court's holding that the police performed an illegal search by spying on a curtilage garden from the air, there was, and is, *no remedy*, since the action only violated the state constitution but not the federal constitution.

Cannabis Gardens on Public Property

IN recent years, it has become increasingly common for people to grow Cannabis on public lands. The legal advantage of such gardening is that it makes it more difficult for the prosecutor to link the plants to a specific person. Therefore, although the police often locate these secluded Cannabis gardens and destroy the plants, they often are unable to prosecute the grower. As a result, the grower loses the plants, but is only rarely subjected to an arrest or search. That is not always the case, however.

Michael Weiss and his son Jeffrey had established a 30-plant Cannabis garden on secluded public property in the town of Albany, Vermont. One day, unbeknownst to the Weiss's, Vermont State Trooper Whitcomb spotted the garden during an aerial observation of the area. Ten days later Whitcomb and another officer went to the area on foot and discovered the Cannabis plants. The officers searched the area but didn't find anyone.

About one hour later, Whitcomb returned to the garden with two other troopers to uproot the Cannabis plants. When they walked into the garden area, they discovered Michael and Jeffrey Weiss tending the plants. They also found several items that had not been there an hour earlier, including two black plastic garbage bags, a plastic garbage can containing manicured marijuana, a nylon bag with shoulder straps, some pruning shears, and a loaded shotgun. The troopers arrested Jeffrey and his dad. Charges against Jeffrey were subsequently dropped, but his dad was prosecuted. Based on the items found at the garden site, the officers suspected that more evidence could be found at the Weiss home. Therefore, the troopers sought and obtained a search warrant authorizing them to search the home. Inside, the officers found additional incriminating evidence.

Michael Weiss argued that the search warrant was invalid, because it failed to state facts showing probable cause that incriminating evidence would be found at his home. The Vermont Supreme Court disagreed. The court explained that the items found at the public garden site had not been there an hour earlier and that they were the sort of items commonly stored at a household. In the court's words, "the presence of the defendants at the marijuana patch with common household items created a link between the residence and the site sufficient for the court to lawfully authorize the search warrant." Therefore, the court concluded that the search warrant was valid.

The other legal advantage to growing Cannabis on public property is that it provides some additional protection against asset forfeiture. First, the government may be unable to figure out who grew the plants and therefore be unable to seize the grower's assets. Second, even if the police do catch the grower, the grower's own land is not subject to forfeiture, since it was not used to facilitate the crime.

The legal disadvantage of gardening on public property is that the gardener has absolutely no right to attack an illegal search of the garden. Why? Because, as discussed in an earlier section, the courts hold that a person has no reasonable expectation of privacy in land that he has no right to be on. In other words, if you grow Cannabis on public property, or on any property that you have no right to enter, you have no Fourth-Amendment protection against searches by a police officer, even if the officer's search was clearly illegal.

8. What If You're Arrested?

In general, there are only two occasions when a police officer can legally arrest a person: (1) if the officer has an arrest warrant specifically authorizing the arrest of the person, or (2) if the officer has probable cause to believe the person committed a crime. In some states, such as California, an officer can arrest an adult for a misdemeanor only if the crime was committed in the officer's presence. In many states, a juvenile can be arrested for a misdemeanor even though the crime was not committed in the presence of an officer.

Citizen's Arrest

In California, as in most states, a citizen can perform an arrest if he sees another person commit a crime. This is known as a "citizen's arrest." There really is not any difference between a citizen's arrest and a normal arrest. The citizen simply calls the police and tells them what happened. An officer then apprehends the accused and the citizen places him under arrest by signing his ticket or notice to appear in court. Alternatively, the citizen can physically detain the person until the police arrive.

Arrest Warrants

Very few arrests for marijuana occur with an arrest warrant, so the subject will be discussed only briefly. Generally speaking, an arrest warrant is just like a search warrant. An arrest warrant is issued by a judge after a police officer presents him with an affidavit showing probable cause that a particular person committed a crime and can be found in his home. The officer then takes the warrant to the person's home and arrests the person.

About the only time a police officer needs an arrest warrant to arrest a person is when he seeks to arrest the person inside his own home. No warrant is needed to arrest a person outside his home in a public place, as long as the officer has probable cause to believe that the person committed a crime.

Officers are well aware of the above rules, and will often try to trick a person into leaving his or her house, so that the officer can arrest the person without an arrest warrant. For example, there are numerous cases in which police officers who have no arrest warrant go to a person's home in the hopes of arresting the person. The officers knock on the door and, when the person answers, ask him to step outside so they can talk to him. As soon as the person steps out the door, the officers can, and do, lawfully arrest him. This is another good reason why you should never open your door to a police officer who does not have either a search warrant or an arrest warrant.

If Arrested Outside, Don't Go Inside!

THE United States Supreme Court has held that if a lawfully arrested person requests to enter his home before being taken to jail, the arresting officers have a legal right to accompany the person inside the residence. This rule was created by the Court after police officers arrested Carl Overdahl, a student at Washington State University. The officers arrested Carl because they observed him leave his dormitory carrying a half-gallon bottle of gin, in violation of the Washington state law forbidding minors to possess alcohol. After Carl was arrested, he asked to return to his dorm room to get his identification, and the officer agreed. When Carl entered his dorm room, the officer also entered and observed in plain view what he believed were marijuana seeds as well as a sea-shell pipe of the type used to smoke marijuana. The officer examined the seeds and confirmed that they were Cannabis, and also confirmed that the pipe smelled of marijuana. At this point, Carl and his roommate Neal confessed that there were three small plastic bags filled with marijuana in the apartment. After they consented to a search, the officers discovered forty grams of marijuana as well as a quantity of LSD.

The Supreme Court stated that once the officers had lawfully arrested Carl, they had a right to follow him into his home after Carl requested to enter. In the Court's words:

> it is not 'unreasonable' under the Fourth Amendment for a police officer, as a matter of routine, to monitor the movements of an arrested person, as his judgment dictates, following the arrest. The officer's need to ensure his own safety—as well as the integrity of the arrest—is compelling. Such a surveillance is not an impermissible invasion of the

privacy or personal liberty of an individual who has been arrested.

The facts in Carl's case are not unusual. In fact, it is quite common for people to ask to return to their home to change into some different clothes before being taken to jail. As in Carl's case, most officers will gladly accommodate such a request, in hopes that they will spot some plain-view contraband once inside the person's home.

In another case, a person was arrested on an outstanding warrant for failing to pay a traffic fine. Before going to jail, the person asked the officers to allow him to go inside to feed his dog. The officers happily agreed. When the officers accompanied the man inside, they detected a very strong odor of marijuana and could see bright lights coming from underneath a closed door in the hallway. Inside the room, the officers discovered forty Cannabis plants.

The obvious lesson to be learned from such cases is that anyone with incriminating evidence in his home, should go directly to jail if arrested. There simply is no reason for returning home to change clothes, get pajamas, or feed gold fish. The jail will provide all the clothing needed, and friends can be called to take care of your pets.

Searches after You're Arrested (The First Exception to the Warrant Requirement)

ONE of the largest exceptions to the search-warrant requirement concerns searches conducted following an arrest. If an officer legally arrests a person, he may conduct a pat-search of the person in order to protect himself. Additionally, as you might imagine, an arrested person is not entitled to much privacy. Therefore, regardless of why the person was arrested, an officer can conduct a full search of a person without first obtaining a search warrant. The only real limit on the search of a person incident to arrest is that the officer cannot conduct a strip search or a body-cavity search simply because a person is arrested. Such searches are, as the Supreme Court has stated, "dehumanizing and humiliating." Therefore the courts will permit such searches only when the officer first obtains a warrant.

Besides searching the person himself, an officer who arrests a person can search the entire area within the person's reach or control. This rule was created to protect law-enforcement officers from persons who, following arrest, lunge for a weapon that was hidden nearby. Therefore an area search conducted incident to a person's arrest is limited to the area of lunging distance. *Any* containers within that area, whether open or closed, can be searched by the officers.

This exception to the search-warrant requirement explains why it is very rare that an officer will get a search warrant that merely authorizes the search of a person. There simply is no need to do so. Why? Because, once an officer has probable cause to believe a person is in possession of marijuana, and the person is in a public place, the officer can simply arrest the person and then legally search him incident to that arrest.

Lastly, whenever the police arrest a person in his home, the police are entitled to search the room in which the person was arrested. The purpose of the search is to confirm that there are no potential attackers hiding in the room. Under this rule, an arresting officer's search is limited to those areas of the room that are large enough to conceal a person; for example, closets. In addition, if the officer reasonably believes that there is someone else anywhere in the arrestee's home, *and* that person poses a danger to the officer, he can search the arrestee's entire home for the person. Remember, under the plain-view rule, any marijuana the officer sees during such a search is seizable and can be admitted in court.

Booking Searches

IF you are booked into jail after an arrest, the police may conduct what is known as a "booking search." The courts have held that warrantless booking searches are justified in order to safeguard people's belongings as well as to keep contraband and weapons out of the jail. During a booking search in most states, an officer may search you and *anything* in your possession. The jail officers can make an item-by-item examination of everything in your pockets or otherwise on your person. They can search your wallet or purse as well as any containers.

Every so often, the police who are booking a person into jail will suspect that an arrestee is concealing drugs or a weapon inside a body cavity. In such cases, most states permit the police to conduct a strip search or a body-cavity search. However, because such searches invade the very core of a person's privacy, most courts have held that the officer must have at least a suspicion that the person is concealing contraband, and his suspicion must be a reasonable one. Some courts go further and require probable cause. In no states can an officer automatically perform a strip or body-cavity search just because he's arrested a person.

Additionally, some states, such as California, have further rules regulating strip and body-cavity searches. For example, in California, a search warrant is required before an officer can perform a strip or body-cavity search of a person arrested for a misdemeanor. Additionally, the search must be conducted in private by a licensed medical personnel who is of the same gender as the arrestee.

Your Miranda Rights

IF you are arrested, it is quite likely that a police officer will "read you your rights" as follows:

> You have the right to remain silent. Anything you say can and will be used against you in court. You have the right to an attorney and to have the attorney present during questioning. If you cannot afford an attorney, one will be appointed for you. Do you understand and waive these rights?"

The above statement of some of your constitutional rights is commonly called your "Miranda rights," named after a defendant in a case. In that case, Mr. Miranda was arrested and taken to the police station for questioning. The officers questioned him in a small room without advising him of his right to an attorney or his right to remain silent. The questioning resulted in Mr. Miranda confessing to a crime.

The Supreme Court Discloses
Police Interrogation Techniques

THE Miranda case is important not only because it was the case in which the Supreme Court created the above-described rule, but also because the justices of the Supreme Court took the opportunity to extensively document some of the interrogation techniques taught to police officers. Although the opinion was written in 1966, some of the interrogation techniques described are still in use today. It is important to understand that the Court's ruling did *not* outlaw the use of the interrogation techniques described below. Rather, the Court held that whenever a person is questioned while in custody, the person must be advised of his right to remain silent and of his right to counsel. In order to give an insight into police interrogation techniques, a portion of the Supreme Court's actual opinion in the Miranda case is quoted below:

An understanding of the nature and setting of this in-custody interrogation is essential to our decisions today. The difficulty in depicting what transpires at such interrogations stems from the fact that in this country they have largely taken place incommunicado. From extensive factual studies undertaken in the early 1930s, including the famous Wickersham Report to Congress by a Presidential Commission, it is clear that police violence and the "third degree" flourished at that time. In a series of cases decided by this Court long after these studies, the police resorted to physical brutality—beatings, hanging, whipping—and to sustained and protracted questioning incommunicado in order to extort confessions. The Commission on Civil Rights in 1961 found much evidence to indicate that "some policemen still resort to physical force to obtain confessions." The use of physical brutality and violence is not, unfortunately, relegated to the past or to any part of the country. Only recently in Kings County, New York, the police brutally beat, kicked, and placed lighted cigarette butts on the back of a potential witness under interrogation for the purpose of securing a statement incriminating a third party.

Interrogation still takes place in privacy. Privacy results in secrecy and this in turn results in a gap in our knowledge as to what in fact goes on in the interrogation rooms. A valuable source of information about present police practices, however, may be found in various police manuals and texts that document procedures employed with success in the past, and that recommend various other effective tactics. These texts are used by law-enforcement agencies themselves as guides. It should be noted that these texts professedly present the most enlightened and effective means presently used to obtain statements through custodial interrogation. By considering these texts and other data, it is possible to describe procedures observed and noted around the country.

The officers are told by the manuals that the "principal psychological factor contributing to a successful interrogation is privacy—being alone with the person under interrogation." The efficacy of this tactic has been explained as follows:

"If at all practicable, the interrogation should take place in the investigator's office or at least in a room of his own choice. The subject should be deprived of every psychological advantage. In his own home he may be confident, indignant, or recalcitrant. He is more keenly aware of his rights and more reluctant to tell of his indiscretions or criminal behavior within the walls of his home. Moreover his family and other friends are nearby, their presence lending moral support. In his office, the investigator possesses all the advantages. The atmosphere suggests the invincibility of the forces of the law."

To highlight the isolation and unfamiliar surroundings, the manuals instruct the police to display an air of confidence in the suspect's guilt and from outward appearance to maintain only an interest in confirming certain details. The guilt of the subject is to be posited as a fact. The interrogator should direct his comments toward the reasons why the subject committed the act, rather than court failure by asking the subject whether he did it. Like other men, perhaps the subject has had a bad family life, had an unhappy childhood, had too much to drink, had an unrequited desire for women. The officers are instructed to minimize the moral seriousness of the offense, to cast blame on the victim or on society. These tactics are designed to put the subject in a psychological state where his story is but an elaboration of what the police purport to know already—that he is guilty. Explanations to the contrary are dismissed and discouraged.

The texts thus stress that the major qualities an interrogator should possess are patience and perseverance. One writer describes the efficacy of these characteristics in this manner:

"In the preceding paragraphs emphasis has been placed on kindness and stratagems. The investigator will, however, encounter many situations where the sheer weight of his personality will be the deciding factor. Where emotional appeals and tricks are employed to no avail, he must rely on an oppressive atmosphere of dogged persistence. He must interrogate steadily and without relent, leaving the subject no prospect of surcease. He must dominate his subject and overwhelm him with his inexorable will to obtain the truth. He should interrogate for a spell of several hours pausing only for the subject's necessities in acknowledgment of the need to avoid a charge of duress that can be technically substantiated. In a serious case, the interrogation may continue for days, with the required intervals for food and sleep, but with no respite from the atmosphere of domination. It is possible in this way to induce the subject to talk without resorting to duress or coercion. The method should be used only when the guilt of the subject appears highly probable."

The manuals suggest that the suspect be offered legal excuses for his actions in order to obtain an initial admission of guilt. Where there is a suspected revenge-killing, for example, the interrogator may say:

"Joe, you probably didn't go out looking for this fellow with the purpose of shooting him. My guess is, however, that you expected something from him and that's why you carried a gun—for your own protection. You know him for what he was, no good. Then when you met him he probably started using foul, abusive language and he gave some indication that he was about to pull a gun on you, and that's when you had to act to save your own life. That's about it, isn't it, Joe?"

Having then obtained the admission of shooting, the interrogator is advised to refer to circumstantial evidence that negates the self-defense explanation. This should enable him to secure the entire story. One text notes that "Even if he fails to do so, the inconsistency between the subject's original denial of the shooting and his present admission of at least doing the shooting will serve to deprive him of a self-defense 'out' at the time of trial."

When the techniques described above prove unavailing, the texts recommend they be alternated with a show of some hostility. One ploy often used has been termed the "friendly-unfriendly" or the "Mutt and Jeff" act:

". . . . In this technique, two agents are employed. Mutt, the relentless investigator, who knows the subject is guilty and is not going to waste any time. He's sent a dozen men away for this crime and he's going to send the subject away for the full term. Jeff, on the other hand, is obviously a kindhearted man. He has a family himself. He has a brother who was involved in a little scrape like this. He disapproves of Mutt and his tactics and will arrange to get him off the case if the subject will cooperate. He can't hold Mutt off for very long. The subject would be wise to make a quick decision. The technique is applied by having both investigators present while Mutt acts out his role. Jeff may stand by quietly and demur at some of Mutt's tactics. When Jeff makes his plea for cooperation, Mutt is not present in the room."

The interrogators sometimes are instructed to induce a confession out of trickery. The technique here is quite effective in crimes which require identification or which run in series. In the identification situation, the interrogator may take a break in his questioning to place the subject among a group of men in a line-up. "The witness or complainant (previously coached, if necessary) studies the line-up and confidently points out the subject as the guilty party." Then the questioning resumes "as though there were no doubt about the guilt of the subject." A variation on this technique is called the "reverse line-up":

"The accused is placed in a line-up, but this time he is identified by several fictitious witnesses or victims who associated him with different offenses. It is expected that the subject will become desperate and confess to the offense under investigation in order to escape from the false accusations."

The manuals also contain instructions for police on how to handle the individual who refuses to discuss the matter entirely, or who asks for an attorney or relatives. The examiner is to concede him the right to remain silent. "This usually has a very undermining effect. First of all, he is disappointed in his expectation of an unfavorable reaction on the part of the interrogator. Secondly, a concession of this right to remain silent impresses the subject with the apparent fairness of his interrogator." After this psychological conditioning, however, the officer is told to point out the incriminating significance of the suspect's refusal to talk:

"Joe, you have a right to remain silent. That's your privilege and I'm the last person in the world who'll try to take it away from you. If that's the way you want to leave this, O.K. But let me ask you this. Suppose you were in my shoes and I were in yours and you called me in to ask me about this and I told you, 'I don't want to answer any of your questions.' You'd think I had something to hide, and you'd probably be right in thinking that. That's exactly what I'll have to think about you, and so will everybody else. So let's sit here and talk this whole thing over."

Few will persist in their initial refusal to talk, it is said, if this monologue is employed correctly.

When the Police Must Read You Your Rights

Most people who learn their law from watching television believe that any time a police officer arrests a person, the officer must immediately read the person his Miranda rights. Other people believe that any time a police officer questions a person, the officer must first read him his rights. In fact, however, both beliefs are widespread myths evidencing a misunderstanding of a very important constitutional right.

The truth is that the only time an officer must read a person his or her Miranda rights is when: (1) the person has been taken into custody, *and* (2) the officer is about to question the person about a crime.

Therefore, if you walk into a police station and state that you want to make a confession the officers are not required to read you your rights before taking your confession. However, in this situation, most officers will read you your rights just to be safe, or because they don't understand the law. Likewise, if an officer walks up to you as you leave your backyard garden and asks you what you are growing, he need not read you your rights before you answer. In both of these examples, you are not in custody; so any information you volunteer to the officer will be admissible, despite the fact that you were never read your rights.

As a final note, your Fifth-Amendment right against forced self-incrimination extends only to "testimony." The courts have defined "testimony" very narrowly, as only spoken words. Therefore the Fifth Amendment does not protect you against self-incrimination based on the taking of your blood or body fluids.

It's Rarely Wise to Waive Your Miranda Rights

It generally takes a police officer about ten seconds to read your Miranda rights and ask if you agree to waive them. The decision to waive these rights, like any constitutional rights, should *not* be made hastily. Let's break down what an officer is telling you when he reads you your rights.

First, he is saying that these are your *rights*. As with all the other rights discussed in this book, you should not feel guilty about exercising your Miranda rights. Your constitutional rights protect you whether innocent or guilty. The first right an officer informs you of is your right to remain silent. This right was deemed of such importance that it was included in the Fifth Amendment to the U.S. Constitution. The Fifth Amendment is usually said to protect a person from forced self-incrimination. In practice, the Fifth Amendment permits a person to remain silent when interrogated by police officers or questioned in court. In addition, the United States Supreme Court has held that if a person exercises his or her Fifth-Amendment right and refuses to answer a police officer's questions, this fact cannot be used against the person in court.

In other words, it is improper for the prosecution to comment on the fact that a person refused to answer a cop's questions. In fact, many cases have been reversed because of a prosecutor's comment, such as, "Ladies and gentlemen, if the defendant was really innocent, wouldn't he have answered all the questions the police asked? Wouldn't he take the opportunity to explain his innocence?" There is no reason to worry that your failure to answer the officer's questions will later be used against you. The truth is that *anything* you *say* will be used against you. Also, don't make the mistake of thinking that only *written* statements can be used against you. To repeat, *anything* you say, whether oral, written, taped, not taped, signed or not signed, will be used against you if the statement benefits the prosecutor's case.

Knowing that anything you say to a police officer will be used against you, why would you want to make a confession or answer questions? In just about every case imaginable, a person is best off not answering any questions about his involvement in criminal activity. The only time when it is wise to answer an officer's questions, once you're in custody, is when you are absolutely innocent of any criminal activity. In that situation, carefully answering the officer's questions may result in your quick release. However, you must be very careful not to let the officer put words in your mouth.

The second right that an officer informs you of is your right to an attorney. If you are unable to afford an attorney, the court must appoint the Public Defender or a private attorney. This is a very important right, and is based on the Fifth and Sixth Amendments. Again, you should never feel shy about exercising this right. If you request an attorney, the police officer must immediately stop questioning you and may not resume until an attorney is present.

The best way to assert your Miranda rights is to say these exact words: "I want an attorney and will remain silent until one is provided." The United States Supreme Court has held that this statement cloaks a person with the protection of both the Fifth and the Sixth Amendments, and hence provides the person with the maximum protection available under the Constitution.

Generally, the last thing an officer says when he reads you your rights is, "Do you understand and agree to waive these rights?" As you can see, the sentence is actually two separate questions. However, many police officers ask it as quoted above, rather than break it down into the two separate questions. When the questions are combined, most people hear only the first portion of the question and answer "yes," not fully realizing that they have just waived some of their most cherished constitutional rights. Of course, it is very important to know that you can always invoke your Miranda rights even after you have waived them (even if the waiver was in writing). You need only say that you now wish to remain silent or have a lawyer. Such a statement should stop the questioning immediately, despite the earlier waiver and despite the fact that you have already answered some questions.

How to Clean Up a Marijuana Conviction Record

WELL, lets say the worst has happened, and you've been convicted of a marijuana offense. Is there anything you can do to make it all better? Well, in some states, for certain marijuana convictions, the answer is "yes."

For example, in California, if, *after* December 31, 1975, you were arrested or convicted of either (1) possession of any amount of marijuana (but not for sale), or (2) offering to transport, transporting, offering to give away, or giving away, less than an ounce of marijuana, then your arrest/conviction record will automatically be destroyed two years after your arrest or conviction! This, of course, happens only if you successfully complete all the terms of your sentence.

If your marijuana arrest or conviction occurred *prior* to January 1, 1976, you can still get your records destroyed, but it is slightly more difficult, and will cost you a few dollars. Here's the rule: If prior to January 1, 1976, you were arrested or convicted of either (1) possession of any amount of marijuana (but not for sale), or (2) possession of paraphernalia used to smoke marijuana, or (3) visiting or being present in a place where marijuana was being used, or (4) being under the influence of marijuana, you can get your records destroyed by submitting a simple form to the Department of Justice.

The form is very simple to fill out, and can be obtained from any police or sheriff's station, or by writing or calling the California Department of Justice. Tell them you want the form titled "Application to Destroy Arrest/Conviction Records" and that this is pursuant to Health and Safety code section 11361.5(b).

Once you get the form, simply fill in the boxes, write a check for $37.50 (as of this writing), and send it off as the form instructs. Occasionally, the D.O.J. has problems finding a person's records, and in such cases requests a copy of your fingerprints within fifteen days. Most defense attorneys advise their clients to go ahead and submit their prints. Others are less trustful, and advise their clients to drop the whole thing if the D.O.J. makes such a request. The decision in such a case is yours.

Assuming everything goes well, the D.O.J. will soon notify you by mail that all records held by the D.O.J., the F.B.I., the local police agency that arrested you, the probation department, and the D.M.V. concerning your arrest/conviction have been destroyed!

Once your records have been destroyed, either automatically or by sending in the form and receiving a confirmation by the D.O.J., you can legally answer that you have never been arrested or convicted for those crimes. Likewise, no public agency can deny you a license because of your arrest/conviction.

9. Defense Attorneys

The Right to Counsel

It should be clear from everything explained in the previous chapters that our criminal-justice system is adversarial. If you are suspected of committing a crime, the resources of the state and/or federal government are marshaled against you. The police will do their best to arrest and question you. Detectives will do their best to gather evidence against you, both physical and testimonial. Forensic scientists employed by the prosecutor will do their best to examine the evidence and relate it to your guilt. At trial, the government is represented by a prosecutor whose goal is to prove, beyond a reasonable doubt, that you are guilty of the crime charged. On the other side of the equation is you, the defendant.

Fortunately, the Sixth Amendment to the United States Constitution states "in all criminal prosecutions, the accused shall enjoy the right to have the assistance of counsel for his defence." The boundaries of the right to counsel have shifted over time. Currently, the Supreme Court has held that, despite the clear language of the Sixth Amendment, the right to counsel does *not* apply in "all" criminal prosecutions. Rather, the Court has held that the right to counsel only extends to cases in which the defendant is *actually* sentenced to jail. Theoretically then, you can be criminally prosecuted and denied the right to counsel so long as the actual punishment you receive is "only" a fine and you receive no jail time. Consequently, in most states, if you are charged with "petty offenses," such as traffic citations, or a marijuana crime that is punishable only by a fine, you may not be entitled to an attorney at the state's expense. Practically speaking, however, most marijuana crimes do carry the potential penalty of imprisonment; hence if you cannot afford an attorney one will be provided.

Public Defenders and Court Appointed Attorneys

Most people who are charged with crimes cannot afford an attorney; so, if the defendant could receive imprisonment as a punishment, the government will provide the defendant with a public defender or a court-appointed attorney.

Public defenders often get a bad rap. Many people believe they are untrained pawns of the government who get paid for walking the defendant through the system to a quick conviction. In my experience this is inaccurate. First, despite the widespread belief to the contrary, public defenders *are attorneys*. They have been to law school and have passed a rigorous exam just like all other attorneys. Additionally, because public defenders who handle misdemeanor cases are often young attorneys just out of law school, they are usually well versed on the latest legal trends and are up-to-date on the rules of law and evidence. Similarly, also because they are often young, many public defenders are enthusiastic about their job and see themselves as legal warriors fighting for the rights of the poor and underprivileged. Such a public defender is often a strong advocate. Lastly, because public defenders handle a large case load of nothing but criminal cases, they are usually very familiar with the local judges and district attorneys, as well as the standard punishment for particular crimes.

Of course, there are some negatives to using a public defender, the biggest being that all public defenders are extremely overworked, often carrying three or four times as many cases as a private attorney would. For that reason, a public defender can rarely spend as much time on your case as a private attorney would. Similarly, if your case is extremely complex, and requires a lot of investigation and expert testimony, the public defender may have difficulty getting an approval to spend the money necessary to do the job properly.

All in all, representation by a public defender is usually better than most people think. Your biggest problem will be getting your public defender to focus on *your* case. Do whatever you can to keep your name and case in the public defender's mind. Don't be afraid to politely, but regularly, check in to get an update on the case. Also, ask him or her what you can do to assist in your defense (for example, try to locate witnesses, take photographs, etc.). The old saying about the squeaky wheel getting the oil is definitely true when it comes to public defenders and their heavy caseload.

In some situations, rather than receive a public defender, you may be provided with a private attorney whose fees are paid by the government. There are two ways this can occur. First, in some counties there is no public-defender organization. Rather, the county maintains a list of private attorneys who are appointed by the court to represent indigent defendants. Therefore, if your county has no public-defender office, you will receive a private court-appointed attorney. The second way to receive a private attorney at little or no cost to you is if your case involves other defendants in addition to yourself. Often in cases with multiple defendants, the court will require each defendant to have his or her own attorney. The public defender can represent one such defendant, but then private attorneys will be appointed to represent the remaining defendants.

As with public defenders, there are good and bad aspects to receiving a court-appointed attorney. On the positive side, most court-appointed attorneys have more time to spend on your case than does the typical public defender. Unlike a public defender, a private court-appointed attorney can turn down cases when he feels he is becoming overburdened. On the negative side, many attorneys who are appointed by the court to handle misdemeanor cases are extremely inexperienced at handling criminal matters. In fact, many counties allow *any* attorney to receive misdemeanor appointments. Many young attorneys who are just starting out in practice apply to receive misdemeanor appointments; so an attorney who has just passed the bar exam, and who has never even been inside a courtroom before, *could* be appointed to handle your misdemeanor case. Fortunately, if you are charged with a felony, most counties will require your appointed attorney to have proven experience in criminal matters. In fact, if you are charged with a felony and given a court-appointed attorney, you may very well get an expensive attorney whom others would pay thousands of dollars to retain.

Choosing a Private Attorney

For people who can hire their own attorney, the selection process can be confusing. If you are charged with a marijuana or other drug crime, you need a trial attorney that handles nothing but criminal cases. You don't want an attorney that handles business matters, divorces, and wills. Such attorneys spend almost all their time drafting legal documents, spend little time in court, and generally have little trial experience. Additionally, although twenty years ago a lawyer could be a general practitioner and remain competent to handle criminal matters, today the criminal laws are so complex and everchanging that a "jack -of-all-trades" lawyer cannot possibly represent you as well as a focused criminal lawyer can.

Again, what you need if charged with a marijuana crime is an attorney who handles *nothing but* criminal cases. If you know a judge or a court bailiff, ask them to recommend a good criminal attorney in your area. Think twice about using an "attorney referral service." Many such services are filled with brand-new attorneys or unsuccessful attorneys scraping to make a living. Ask the service what qualifications an attorney must have to be a member of the service.

For most marijuana cases, it is usually best to retain an attorney who has a solo practice or is a member of a law firm with no more than 5 lawyers. With a sole practitioner you know who is handling your case and hence who to contact with any new information, or to get an update. Often large law firms have several attorneys work on a file. In theory there should not be a problem with this. In fact, some people like the idea of having several attorneys working together on their case. Such representation may be good if each attorney is interested in your case and effectively communicates his thoughts to the other attorneys working your case. In practice, however, problems often arise because no single person is fully involved, and therefore fully prepared, in all aspects of the case. Likewise, bigger firms often employ paralegals and law clerks to conduct legal research and to prepare many of the legal motions and memoranda filed in court. Why pay a big firm to handle your case when a paralegal is doing much of the work?

Criminal defense attorneys can be located by thumbing through the yellow pages, or by asking around to your friends. When looking through the yellow pages, you will see many criminal defense attorneys who advertise that they began their careers by working for a prosecuting agency before going out on their own. These attorneys are often very experienced. However, I would not recommend such attorneys, simply because their employment history indicates a fundamental ideological flaw: they used to earn a pay check by convicting people who smoke or grow marijuana. Rather than hire such an attorney, look for one who presents himself or herself as ideologically opposed to the government's prosecution of people for marijuana crimes. You want an attorney that really believes in the case he or she is fighting for. Such an attorney is more enthusiastic, a harder worker, and often more effective. Therefore look for someone that has never worked for the government as a prosecutor. Prior experience as a public defender is good, because it shows that the lawyer has always cared about defending people.

Once you have selected several attorneys you think might be good, call them and arrange a free consultation. Almost all criminal attorneys will meet with you for free to hear about your case and quote you a fee. Set up several such interviews on a single day and choose the attorney that most impresses you and whose fee you can afford. You should retain the attorney who is enthusiastic about defending you (i.e., not burned out), intelligent, and very well-versed on defending marijuana cases.

10. Drug Testing at Work

As part and parcel of the "war on drugs," many public and private employers are beginning to test their employees, and potential employees, for marijuana and other drug use. At the moment, more than 20 million people are being subjected to drug testing, including most police officers, military personnel, defense contractors, transportation workers, and nearly half the employees who work for Fortune 500 companies.

Your rights with regard to drug testing at work depend primarily upon whether you're employed by the government (or in an industry or profession that's heavily regulated by the government) or privately employed.

Government Employees (and Those Working in Heavily Regulated Industries)

In a relatively recent case, the United States Supreme Court established a test for deciding the constitutionality of drug testing government employees. The Court held that the constitutionality of such government employee drug tests must be decided by applying a balancing test. Under this test, a court must weigh the government's interest or purpose in requiring the drug tests against the employees' reasonable expectation of privacy. The drug test will be legal if the Court concludes that the government's interest outweighed the employees'. When the Court wrote its opinion, it was clear from the outset that employees have a very reasonable expectation of privacy in their own bodily fluids. Indeed, what could be more private? Given the clear and strong privacy expectation, the Court concluded that drug tests of government employees are only constitutional, and hence legal, if the government can show a truly *compelling* interest in requiring an employee to submit to a drug test.

The case itself involved a federal regulation requiring mandatory blood and urine tests of *privately* employed railroad employees who were involved in train accidents. The first question that the Court had to answer was whether a *private* employer's drug test was a "search" under the Fourth Amendment.

The federal government argued that the railroads were all private organizations and that therefore their actions were not regulated by the Constitution. In opposition, the employees argued that although the railroads were indeed private companies, the railroad industry was so heavily regulated by the government that the companies, in effect, acted as the agents of the government. The Court agreed with the employees, finding that the private railroad companies had to follow so many government regulations that they were almost an arm of the government itself! Accordingly, the Court held that the railroads were subject to the Fourth Amendment, and hence any forced drug testing had to comply with the Constitution.

However, the Court then explained that the government has a compelling interest in promoting the safety of rail travel and that this important government interest permitted the government to prohibit railroad employees from using drugs while on duty. Therefore, the Court concluded, the mandatory drug tests were necessary to ensure that railroad employees were abiding by the no-drugs rule. The Court also explained that no search warrants were required to conduct the tests, because such a procedure would hinder the program's effectiveness.

After finding that the testing passed muster under the Fourth Amendment, the Court next addressed the issue of whether some indication that an employee was using drugs was required before an employee could be forced to submit to a drug test. To resolve this question, the Court again resorted to a balancing test. The Court weighed the railroad employees' expectation of privacy against the government's interest in maintaining safe rail travel. The Court concluded that safe rail travel was extremely important and that the industry has always been subject to extreme regulation. Therefore, the Court concluded, an employee can be forced to take a drug test even without any indication that the employee uses drugs.

Subsequent federal cases have upheld random drug testing of probation officers, law-enforcement personnel, military personnel, air-traffic controllers, pilots, aircraft mechanics and attendants, school-bus drivers, nuclear-power-plant workers, and racehorse jockeys. Fortunately, many state courts have interpreted their own state constitution as giving employees greater protection than that offered by the federal constitution. In many such states, a state employee cannot be drug tested without at least a reasonable suspicion that he is using drugs on the job.

Drug Testing of Private Employees

As explained in earlier chapters, the United States Constitution provides you with protections only against actions by the government or its agents; so a private company is not restrained by constitutional protections against unusual searches and seizures. However, many states are now enacting legislation controlling drug testing at work. Some states give private employees pretty good protection. For example, the Connecticut law, which is similar to those in many states, prescribes that an employee can be forced to take a drug test only if there is reasonable suspicion that the employee is under the influence of drugs at work and that the suspected drug use is adversely affecting his job performance. In addition, in order for the company to take a personnel action against the employee, a positive test must be confirmed by two additional tests. Moreover, persons applying for work in Connecticut can be subjected to drug testing as part of the application process only if they are given prior written notification of the test and are provided a copy of any positive results. Most importantly, in Connecticut, any positive test results are considered confidential and *cannot* be used in a criminal proceeding.

The Drug-Free Workplace Act of 1988

In 1988, Congress passed what is commonly known as "The Drug-Free Workplace Act." This law applies to private companies that receive federal contracts worth $25,000 or more. The Act requires these companies to create and publicize an "anti-drug" policy and to create a "drug-free awareness program." In addition, employees of such companies must be notified that they must report any workplace drug offenses that result in their conviction.

Although the Act presently does not explicitly require drug testing of company employees, such an amendment is possible down the road. In addition, it is possible that companies will start drug testing on their own in order to ensure compliance with the Act's intent of providing drug-free workplaces.

What to Expect If You're Drug-Tested at Work

The exact procedures used in employee drug testing will depend on your state, your occupation, and your employer. Usually you can expect roughly the following procedure.

Often drug tests are done not by the company itself, but rather by an independent company that's hired just for that purpose. Accordingly, the people conducting the test have never met the employees and hence will require that you provide proof of your identity. This is to prevent employees from secretly sending drug-free substitutes to take the test for them. Therefore the first step in most drug tests is for the testing company to require some form of photo identification.

Once sufficient evidence of your identity has been presented, the tester will give you a questionnaire form asking you if you have taken any drugs (over-the-counter or prescription) within the last thirty days. If you answer that you have taken a prescription drug, the tester will usually require that you to present them with the prescription or the bottle itself. The tester asks this question because many legal drugs can cause false positive results. For example, one of the most commonly used testing methods, known as EMIT (short for enzyme-multiplied immunoassay technique) can return false positive results for marijuana cannabinoids if the person has recently taken Ibuprofen. Ibuprofen is found in such extremely common pain medications as Advil, Nuprin, Motrin, and Mydol!

Once the questionnaire has been completed, the next step is obtaining the sample. Almost all employee drug testing is done by way of a urine sample. Usually you are allowed to urinate in private, without the tester observing the actual act of urination. However, in some states and with some employers, your urine sample will be given under the watchful eye of an observer. Beware that if you're permitted to urinate in private, the testers will usually place a bluing agent in the toilet to prevent you from diluting your urine sample with fresh water from the toilet.

Once you have filled your container, you will probably be asked to sign a small label to be placed on the container and then to hand it to the tester. The tester will first look at it for any indication that you attempted to dilute it, as just discussed. Next, the tester will take your sample's temperature to make sure it's within the range of a sample that would come out of a human body. If everything looks legitimate, your sample will then be taken to the laboratory for the actual drug analysis. Usually, within two weeks you will learn of the results.

Epilogue

As a practicing criminal-defense attorney, I have become convinced that the constitutional rights created to protect us against runaway government, are being sacrificed in the "War on Drugs." The Cannabis plant is not evil; arbitrary government is. It is time to change our way of thinking about drugs. Long after the hysteria has subsided, we will be left not with a drug-free society, but rather with a less-free society. Constitutional rights are not second-class rights. Rather, as Justice Jackson wrote:

> [Constitutional rights] belong in the catalog of indispensable freedoms. Among deprivations of rights, none is so effective in cowing a population, crushing the spirit of the individual and putting terror in every heart. Uncontrolled search and seizure is one of the first and most effective weapons in the arsenal of every arbitrary government.

If "We the People" are ignorant of our constitutional rights, or unwilling to assert them, they are of no worth. It will be us, not the government, whom is to blame for the resulting society in which few individual freedoms will remain. George Orwell predicted 1984 as the year in which the government became superior to the individual. Unless we rethink our current policy with regard to marijuana and other drugs, Orwell's prediction may turn out to be only slightly premature.

> It was always at night—the arrests invariably happened at night. The sudden jerk out of sleep, the rough hand shaking your shoulder, the lights glaring in your eyes, the ring of hard faces round the bed. In the vast majority of cases there was no trial, no report of the arrest. People simply disappeared, always during the night. Your name was removed from the registers, every record of everything you had ever done was wiped out, your one-time existence was denied and forgotten. You were abolished, annihilated: *vaporized* was the usual word.

Appendix A:
The Bill of Rights

The First Amendment

CONGRESS shall make no law respecting an establishment of religion, or prohibiting the free exercise thereof; or abridging the freedom of speech, or of the press; or the right of the people peaceably to assemble, and to petition the Government for a redress of grievances.

The Second Amendment

A well-regulated Militia being necessary to the security of a free State, the right of the people to keep and bear Arms shall not be infringed.

The Third Amendment

No Soldier shall in time of peace be quartered in any house without consent of the Owner, nor in time of war, but in a manner to be described by law.

The Fourth Amendment

THE right of the people to be secure in their persons, houses, papers, and effects, against unreasonable searches and seizures, shall not be violated, and no Warrants shall issue, but upon probable cause, supported by Oath or affirmation, and particularly describing the place to be searched, and the persons or things to be seized.

The Fifth Amendment

No person shall be held to answer for a capital or otherwise infamous crime, unless on a presentment or indictment of a Grand Jury, except in cases arising in the land or naval forces, or in the Militia, when in actual service in time of War or public danger; nor shall any person be subject for the same offense to be twice put in jeopardy of life or limb; nor shall be compelled in any criminal case to be a witness against himself, nor be deprived of life, liberty, or property, without due process of law; nor shall private property be taken for public use, without just compensation.

The Sixth Amendment

In all criminal prosecutions, the accused shall enjoy the right to a speedy and public trial, by an impartial jury of the State and district wherein the crime shall have been committed, which district shall have been previously ascertained by law, and to be informed of the nature and cause of the accusation; to be confronted with the witnesses against him; to have compulsory process for obtaining witnesses in his favor, and to have the Assistance of Counsel for his defense.

The Seventh Amendment

In Suits at common law, where the value in controversy shall exceed twenty dollars, the right of trial by jury shall be preserved, and no fact tried by a jury shall be otherwise reexamined in any Court of the United States, than according to the rules of the common law.

The Eighth Amendment

Excessive bail shall not be required, nor excessive fines imposed, nor cruel and unusual punishments inflicted.

The Ninth Amendment

The enumeration in the Constitution of certain rights shall not be construed to deny or disparage others retained by the people.

The Tenth Amendment

The powers not delegated to the United States by the Constitution, nor prohibited by it to the States, are reserved to the States respectively, or to the people.

Appendix B: Federal Sentencing Guidelines Manual

Passages Pertinent to Marijuana and Cannabis

Pursuant to the Act, the sentencing court must select a sentence from within the guideline range. If, however, a particular case presents atypical features, the Act allows the court to depart from the guidelines and sentence outside the prescribed range. In that case, the court must specify reasons for departure. If the court sentences within the guideline range, an appellate court may review the sentence to determine whether the guidelines were correctly applied. If the court departs from the guideline range, an appellate court may review the reasonableness of the departure. The Act also abolishes parole, and substantially reduces and restructures good-behavior adjustments.

The sentencing statute permits a court to depart from a guideline-specified sentence only when it finds "an aggravating or mitigating circumstance of a kind, or to a degree, not adequately taken into consideration by the Sentencing Commission in formulating the guidelines that should result in a sentence different from that described." The Commission intends the sentencing courts treat each guideline as carving out a "heartland," a set of typical cases embodying the conduct that each guideline describes. When a court finds an atypical case, one to which a particular guideline linguistically applies but where conduct significantly differs from the norm, the court may consider whether a departure is warranted.

The guidelines work as follows in respect to a first offender. For offense levels one through six, the sentencing court may elect to sentence the offender to probation (with or without confinement conditions) or to a prison term. For offense levels seven through ten, the conditions (community confinement, intermittent confinement, or home detention). For offense levels eleven and twelve, the court must impose at least one-half the minimum confinement sentence in the form of prison confinement, the remainder to be served on supervised release with a condition of community confinement or home detention. The Commission, of course, has not dealt with the single acts of aberrant behavior that still may justify probation at higher offense levels through departures.

1. Unlawful manufacturing, importing, exporting, trafficking, or possession; continuing criminal enterprise.

§2D1.1. Unlawful Manufacturing, Importing, Exporting, or Trafficking (Including Possession with Intent to Commit These Offenses)

(a) *Base Offense Level (apply the greatest):*

(1) 43, if the defendant is convicted under 21 U.S.C. § 841(b)(1)(A), (b)(1)(B), or (b)(1)(C), or 21 U.S.C. § 960(b)(1), (b)(2), or (b)(3), and the offense of conviction establishes that death or serious bodily injury resulted from the use of the substance and that the defendant committed the offense after one or more prior conviction for a similar offense; or

(2) 38, if the defendant is convicted under 21 U.S.C. § 841(b)(1)(A), (b)(1)(B), or (b)(1)(C), or 21 U.S.C. § 960(b)(1), (b)(2), or (b)(3), and the offense of conviction establishes that death or serious bodily injury resulted from the use of the substance; or

(3) the offense level specified in the Drug Quantity Table set forth in subsection (c) below.

(b) *Specific Offense Characteristics*

(1) If a dangerous weapon (including a firearm) was possessed, increase by two levels.

(2) If the defendant is convicted of violating 21 U.S.C. § 960(a) under circumstances in which (A) an aircraft other than a regularly scheduled commercial air carrier was used to import the controlled substance, or (B) the defendant acted as pilot, copilot, navigator, flight officer, or any other operation officer aboard any craft or vessel carrying a controlled substance, increase by 2 levels. If the resulting offense level is less than level 26, increase to level 26.

(c) *Drug Quantity Table*

Controlled Substances and Quantity*	Base Offense Level

(1)   Level 42
• 300,000 KG or more of Marihuana;
• 60,000 KG or more of Hashish;
• 6,000 KG or more of Hashish Oil.

(2)   Level 40
• At least 100,000 KG but less than 300,000 KG of Marihuana;
• At least 20,000 KG but less than 60,000 KG of Hashish;
• At least 2,000 KG but less than 6,000 KG of Hashish Oil.

(3)   Level 38
• At least 30,000 KG but less than 100,000 KG of Marihuana;
• At least 6,000 KG but less than 20,000 KG of Hashish;
• At least 600 KG but less than 2,000 KG of Hashish Oil.

(4)   Level 36
• At least 10,000 KG but less than 30,000 KG of Marihuana;
• At least 2,000 KG but less than 6,000 KG of Hashish;
• At least 200 KG but less than 600 KG of Hashish Oil.

(5)   Level 34
• At least 3,000 KG but less than 10,000 KG of Marihuana;
• At least 600 KG but less than 2,000 KG of Hashish;
• At least 60 KG but less than 200 KG of Hashish Oil.

(6)   Level 32
• At least 1,000 KG but less than 3,000 KG of Marihuana;
• At least 200 KG but less than 600 KG of Hashish;
• At least 20 KG but less than 60 KG of Hashish Oil.

(7)   Level 30
• At least 700 KG but less than 1,000 KG of Marihuana;
• At least 140 KG but less than 200 KG of Hashish;
• At least 14 KG but less than 20 KG of Hashish Oil.

(8)   Level 28
• At least 400 KG but less than 700 KG of Marihuana;
• At least 80 KG but less than 140 KG of Hashish;
• At least 8 KG but less than 14 KG of Hashish Oil.

(9)   Level 26
• At least 100 KG but less than 400 KG of Marihuana;
• At least 20 KG but less than 80 KG of Hashish;
• At least 2 KG but less than 8 KG of Hashish Oil.

(10)   Level 24
• At least 80 KG but less than 100 KG of Marihuana;
• At least 16 KG but less than 20 KG of Hashish;
• At least 1.6 KG but less than 2 KG of Hashish Oil.

(11)   Level 22
• At least 60 KG but less than 80 KG of Marihuana;
• At least 12 KG but less than 16 KG of Hashish;
• At least 1.2 KG but less than 1.6 KG of Hashish Oil.

(12)   Level 20
• At least 40 KG but less than 60 KG of Marihuana;
• At least 8 KG but less than 12 KG of Hashish;
• At least 800 G but less than 1.2 KG of Hashish Oil.

(13)   Level 18
• At least 20 KG but less than 40 KG of Marihuana;
• At least 5 KG but less than 8 KG of Hashish;
• At least 500 G but less than 800 G of Hashish Oil.

(14)   Level 16
• At least 10 KG but less than 20 KG of Marihuana;
• At least 2 KG but less than 5 KG of Hashish;
• At least 200 G but less than 500 G of Hashish Oil.

(15)   Level 14
• At least 5 KG but less than 10 KG of Marihuana;
• At least 1 KG but less than 2 KG of Hashish;
• At least 100 G but less than 200 G of Hashish Oil.

(16)   Level 12
• At least 2.5 KG but less than 5 KG of Marihuana;
• At least 500 G but less than 1 KG of Hashish;
• At least 50 G but less than 100 G of Hashish Oil.

(17)   Level 10
• At least 1 KG but less than 2.5 KG of Marihuana;
• At least 200 G but less than 500 G of Hashish;
• At least 20 G but less than 50 G of Hashish Oil.

(18)   Level 8
• At least 250 G but less than 1 KG of Marihuana;
• At least 50 G but less than 200 G of Hashish;
• At least 5 G but less than 20 G of Hashish Oil.

(19)   Level 6
• Less than 250 G of Marihuana;
• Less than 50 G of Hashish;
• Less than 5 G of Hashish Oil.

* Unless otherwise specified, the weight of a controlled substance set forth in
the table refers to the entire weight of any mixture or substance containing a
detectable amount of the controlled substance. If a mixture or substance contains
more than one controlled substance, the weight of the entire mixture or substance
is assigned to the controlled substance that results in the greater offense.

In the case of an offense involving marihuana plants, if the offense involved (A) 50 or more marihuana plants, treat each plant as equivalent to 1 KG of marihuana; (B) Fewer than 50 marihuana plants, treat each plant as equivalent to 100 G of marihuana. Provided, however, that if the actual weight of the marihuana is greater, use the actual weight of the marihuana.

Distribution of a "small amount of marihuana for no renumeration", 21 U.S.C. § 841(b)(4), is treated as simple possession, to which §2D2.1 applies.

To facilitate conversions to drug equivalencies, the following table is provided:

Measurement Conversion Table

1 oz = 28.35 gm
1 lb = 453.6 gm
1 lb = 0.4536 kg
1 kg = 1,000 gm
1 gm = 1,000 mg
1 grain = 64.8 mg

Typical Weight per Unit (Dose, Pill, or Capsule)

Marihuana

1 marihuana cigarette	0.5 gm

In cases involving fifty or more marihuana plants, an equivalency of one plant to one kilogram of marihuana is derived from the statutory penalty provisions of 21 U.S.C. § 841(b)(1)(A), (B), and (D). In cases involving fewer than fifty plants, the statute is silent as to the equivalency. For cases involving fewer than fifty plants, the Commission has adopted an equivalency of 100 grams per plant, or the actual weight of the usable marihuana, whichever is greater. The decision to treat each plant as equal to 100 grams is premised on the fact that the average yield from a mature marihuana plant equals 100 grams of marihuana. In controlled substance offenses, an attempt is assigned the same offense level as the object of the attempt (see §2D1.4). Consequently, the Commission adopted the policy that, in the case of fewer than fifty marihuana plants, each plant is to be treated as the equivalent of an attempt to produce 100 grams of marihuana, except where the actual weight of the usable marihuana is greater.

§2D1.4. Attempts and Conspiracies

(a) *Base Offense Level*: If a defendant is convicted of a conspiracy or an attempt to commit any offense involving a controlled substance, the offense level shall be the same as if the object of the conspiracy or attempt has been completed.

Application Notes:

1. If the defendant is convicted of a conspiracy that includes transactions in controlled substances in addition to those that are the subject of substantive counts of conviction, each conspiracy transaction shall be included with those of the substantive counts of conviction to determine scale. If the defendant is convicted of an offense involving negotiation to traffic in a controlled substance, the weight under negotiation in an uncompleted distribution shall be used to calculate the applicable amount. However, where the court finds that the defendant did not intend to produce and was not reasonably capable of producing the negotiated amount, the court shall exclude from the guideline calculation the amount that it finds the defendant did not intend to produce and was not reasonably capable of producing. If the defendant is convicted of conspiracy.

2. Where there is no drug seizure or the amount seized does not reflect the scale of the offense, the sentencing judge shall approximate the quantity of the controlled substance. In making this determination, the judge may consider, for example, the price generally obtained for the controlled substance, financial or other records, similar transactions in controlled substances by the defendant, and the size or capability of any laboratory involved.

2. Unlawful Possession

§2D2.1. Unlawful Possession

(a) *Base Offense Level*:

(3) 4, if the substance is any other controlled substance.

Part A—Criminal History
Introductory Commentary

The Comprehensive Crime Control Act sets forth four purposes of sentencing. A defendant's record of past criminal conduct is directly relevant to those purposes. A defendant with a record of prior criminal behavior is more culpable than a first offender and thus deserving of greater punishment. General deterrence of criminal conduct dictates that a clear message be sent to society that repeated criminal behavior will aggravate the need for punishment with each recurrence. To protect the public from further crimes of the particular defendant, the likelihood of recidivism and future criminal behavior must be considered. Repeated criminal behavior is an indicator of a limited likelihood of successful rehabilitation.

§4A1.1. Criminal History Category

The total points from items (a) through (f) determine the criminal history in the Sentencing Table in Chapter Five, Part A.

> (a) Add 3 points for each prior sentence of imprisonment exceeding one year and one month.
>
> (b) Add 2 points for each prior sentence of imprisonment of at least sixty days not counted in (a).
>
> (c) Add 1 point for each prior sentence not counted in (a) or (b), up to a total of 4 points for this item.
>
> (d) Add 2 points if the defendant committed the instant offense while under any criminal justice sentence, including probation, parole, supervised release, imprisonment, work release, or escape status.
>
> (e) Add 2 points if the defendant committed the instant offense less than two years after release from imprisonment on a sentence counted under (a) or (b) or while in imprisonment or escape status on such a sentence. If 2 points are added for item (d), add only 1 point for this item.
>
> (f) Add 1 point for each prior sentence resulting from a conviction of a crime of violence that did not receive any points under (a), (b), or (c) above because such sentence was considered related to another sentence resulting from a conviction of a crime of violence, up to a total of 3 points for this item. Provided, that this item does not apply where the sentences are considered related because the offenses occurred on the same occasion.

Determining the Sentence

Introductory Commentary

For certain categories of offenses and offenders, the guidelines permit the court to impose either imprisonment or some other sanction or combination of sanctions. In determining the type of sentence to impose, the sentencing judge should consider the nature and seriousness of the conduct, the statuary purposes of sentencing, and the pertinent offender characteristics. A sentence is within the guidelines if it complies with each applicable section of this chapter. The court should impose a sentence sufficient, but not greater than necessary, to comply with the statutory purposes or sentencing.

Sentencing Guidelines
The Sentencing Table used to determineing the guideline range follows:

Sentencing Table
(in months of imprisonment)
Criminal History Category (Criminal History Points)

Offense Level	I (0 or 1)	II (2 or 3)	III (4, 5, 6)	IV (7, 8, 9)	V (10,11,12)	VI (13 or more)
1	0–6	0–6	0–6	0–6	0–6	0–6
2	0–6	0–6	0–6	0–6	0–6	1–7
3	0–6	0–6	0–6	0–6	2–8	3–9
4	0–6	0–6	0–6	2–8	4–10	6–12
5	0–6	0–6	1–7	4–10	6–12	9–15
6	0–6	1–7	2–8	6–12	9–15	12–18
7	1–7	2–8	4–10	8–14	12–18	15–21
8	2–8	4–10	6–12	10–16	15–21	18–24
9	4–10	6–12	8–14	12–18	18–24	21–27
10	6–12	8–14	10–16	15–21	21–27	24–30
11	8–14	10–16	12–18	18–24	24–30	27–33
12	10–16	12–18	15–21	21–27	27–33	30–37
13	12–18	15–21	18–24	24–30	30–37	33–41
14	15–21	18–24	21–27	27–33	33–41	37–46
15	18–24	21–27	24–30	30–37	37–46	41–51
16	21–27	24–30	27–33	33–41	41–51	46–57
17	24–30	27–33	30–37	37–46	46–57	51–63
18	27–33	30–37	33–41	41–51	51–63	57–71
19	30–37	33–41	37–46	46–57	57–71	63–78
20	33–41	37–46	41–51	51–63	63–78	70–87
21	37–46	41–51	46–57	57–71	70–87	77–96

Sentencing Table (continued)

Offense Level	I (0 or 1)	II (2 or 3)	III (4, 5, 6)	IV (7, 8, 9)	V (10,11,12)	VI (13 or more)
22	41–51	46–57	51–63	63–78	77–96	84–105
23	46–57	51–63	57–71	70–87	84–105	92–115
24	51–63	57–71	63–78	77–96	92–115	100–125
25	57–71	63–78	70–87	84–105	100–125	110–137
26	63–78	70–87	78–97	92–115	110–137	120–150
27	70–87	78–97	87–108	100–125	120–150	130–162
28	78–97	87–108	97–121	110–137	130–162	140–175
29	87–108	97–121	108–135	121–151	140–175	151–188
30	97–121	108–135	121–151	135–168	151–188	168–210
31	108–135	121–151	135–168	151–188	168–210	188–235
32	121–151	135–168	151–188	168–210	188–235	210–262
33	135–168	151–188	168–210	188–235	210–262	235–293
34	151–188	168–210	188–235	210–262	235–293	262–327
35	168–210	188–235	210–262	235–293	262–327	292–365
36	188–235	210–262	235–293	262–327	292–365	324–405
37	210–262	235–293	262–327	292–365	324–405	360–life
38	235–293	262–327	292–365	324–405	360–life	360–life
39	262–327	292–365	324–405	360–life	360–life	360–life
40	292–365	324–405	360–life	360–life	360–life	360–life
41	324–405	360–life	360–life	360–life	360–life	360–life
42	360–life	360–life	360–life	360–life	360–life	360–life
43	life	life	life	life	life	life

Commentary to Sentencing Table

Application Notes:

1. The Offense Level (1–43) forms the vertical axis of the Sentencing Table. The Criminal History Category (I–VI) forms the horizontal axis of the Table. The intersection of the Offense Level and Criminal

History Category displays the Guideline Range in months of imprisonment. "Life" means life imprisonment. For example, the guideline range applicable to a defendant with an Offense Level of 15 and a Criminal History Category of III is 24–30 months of imprisonment.

2. In rare cases, a total offense level of less than 1 or more than 43 may result from application of the guidelines. A total offense level of less than 1 is to be treated as an offense level 1. An offense level more than 43 is to be treated as an offense level 43.

3. The Criminal History Category is determined by the total criminal history points from Chapter Four, Part A, except as provided in §§4B1.1 (Career Offender) and 4B1.4 (Armed Career Criminal). The total criminal history points associated with each Criminal History Category are shown under each Criminal History Category in the Sentencing Table.

§5E1.2. Fines for Individual Defendants

(a) The court shall impose a fine in all cases, except where the defendant establishes that he is unable to pay and is not likely to become able to pay any fine.

(b) Except as provided in subsections (f) and (i) below, or otherwise required by statute, the fine imposed shall be within the range specified in subsection (c) below. If, however, the guideline for the offense in Chapter Two provides a specific rule for imposing a fine, that rule takes precedence over subsection (c) of this section.

(c)   (1) The minimum of the fine range is the amount shown in column A of the table below.

(2) Except as specified in (4) below, the maximum of the fine range is the amount shown in column B of the table below.

(3) Fine Table

Offense Level	A Minimum	B Maximum
3 and below	$100	$5,000
4–5	$250	$5,000
6–7	$500	$5,000

Fine Table (continued)

Offense Level	A Minimum	B Maximum
8–9	$1,000	$10,000
10–11	$2,000	$20,000
12–13	$3,000	$30,000
14–15	$4,000	$40,000
16–17	$5,000	$50,000
18–19	$6,000	$60,000
20–22	$7,500	$75,000
23–25	$10,000	$100,000
26–28	$12,500	$125,000
29–31	$15,000	$150,000
32–34	$17,500	$175,000
35–37	$20,000	$200,000
38 & above	$25,000	$250,000

(4)   Subsection (c)(2), limiting the maximum fine, does not apply if the defendant is convicted under a statute authorizing (A) a maximum fine greater than $250,000, or (B) a fine for each day of violation. In such cases, the court may impose a fine up to the maximum authorized by the statute.

(d) In determining the amount of the fine, the court shall consider:

(1)   the need for the combined sentence to reflect the seriousness of the offense (including the harm or loss to the victim and the gain to the defendant), to promote respect for the law, to provide just punishment and to afford adequate deterence.

(2)   any evidence presented as to the defendant's ability to pay the fine (including the ability to pay over a period of time) in light of his earning capacity and financial resources;

(3)   the burden that the fine places on the defendant and his dependents relative to alternative punishments;

(4)   any restitution or reparation that the defendant has made or is obligated to make;

(5)   any collateral consequences of conviction, including civil obligations arising from the defendant's conduct;

    (6)   whether the defendant previously has been fined for a similar offense; and

    (7)   any other pertinent equitable considerations.

(e) The amount of the fine should always be sufficient to ensure that the fine, taken together with other sanctions imposed, is punitive.

(f) If the defendant establishes that (1) he is not able and, even with the use of a reasonable installment schedule, is not likely to become able to pay all or part of the fine required by the preceding provisions, or (2) imposition of a fine would unduly burden the defendant's dependents, the court may impose a lesser fine or waive the fine. In these circumstances, the court shall consider alternative sanctions in lieu of all or a portion of the fine, and must still impose a total combined sanction that is punitive. Although any additional sanction not proscribed by the guidelines is permissible, community service is the generally preferable alternative in such instances.

(g) If the defendant establishes that payment of the fine in a lump sum would have an unduly severe impact on him or his dependents, the court should establish an installment schedule for payment of the fine. The length of the installment schedule generally should not exceed twelve months, and shall not exceed the maximum term of probation authorized for the offense. The defendant should be required to pay a substantial installment at the time of sentencing. If the court authorizes a defendant sentenced to probation or supervised release to pay a fine on an installment schedule, the court shall require as a condition of probation or supervised release that the defendant pay the fine according to the schedule. The court also may impose a condition prohibiting the defendant from incurring new credit charges or opening additional lines of credit unless he is in compliance with the payment schedule.

(h) If the defendant knowingly fails to pay a delinquent fine, the court shall resentence him in accordance with 18 U.S.C. § 3614.

(i) Notwithstanding of the provisions of subsection (c) of this section, but subject to the provisions of subsection (f) herein, the court shall impose an additional fine amount that is at least sufficient to pay the costs to the government of any imprisonment, probation, or supervised release ordered.

Commentary

Application Notes:

1. A fine may be the sole sanction if the guidelines do not require a term of imprisonment. If, however, the fine is not paid in full at the time of sentencing, it is recommended that the court sentence the defendant to a term of probation, with payment of the fine as a condition of probation. If a fine is imposed in addition to a term of imprisonment, it is recommended that the court impose a term of supervised release following imprisonment as a means of enforcing payment of the fine.

2. In general, the maximum fine permitted by law as to each count of conviction is $250,000 for a felony or for any misdemeanor resulting in death; $100,000 for a Class A misdemeanor; and $5,000 for any other offense. 18 U.S.C. § 3571(b)(3)–(7). However, higher or lower limits may apply when specified by statute. 18 U.S.C. § 3571(b)1, (e). As an alternative maximum, the court may fine the defendant up to the greater of twice the gross gain or twice the gross loss. 18 U.S.C. § 3571(b)(2), (d).

3. The determination of the fine guideline range may be dispensed with entirely upon a court determination of present and future inability to pay any fine. The inability of a defendant to post bail bond (having otherwise been determined eligible for release) and the fact that a defendant is represented by (or was determined eligible for) assigned counsel are significant indicators of present inability to pay any fine. In conjunction with other factors, they may also indicate that the defendant is not likely to become able to pay any fine.

4. The Commission envisions that for most defendants, the maximum of the guideline fine range from subsection (c) will be at least twice the amount of gain or loss resulting from the offense. Where, however, two times either the amount of gain to the defendant or the amount of loss caused by the offense exceeds the maximum of the fine guideline, an upward departure from the fine guideline may be warranted. Moreover, where a sentence within the applicable fine guideline range would not be sufficient to ensure both the disgorgement of any gain from the offense that otherwise would not be disgorged (e.g., by restitution or forfeiture) and an adequate punitive fine, an upward departure from the fine guideline range may be warranted.

5. Subsection (c)(4) applies to statutes that contain special provisions permitting larger fines; the guidelines do not limit maximum fines in

such cases. These statutes include, among others: 21 U.S.C. §§ 841(b) and 960(b), which authorized fines up to $8 million in offenses involving the manufacture, distribution, or importation of certain controlled substances; 21 U.S.C. § 848(a), which authorizes fines up to $4 million in offenses involving the manufacture or distribution of controlled substances by a continuing criminal enterprise; 18 U.S.C. § 1956(a), which authorizes a fine equal to the greater of $500,000 or two times the value of the monetary instruments or funds involved in offenses involving money laundering of financial instrument; 18 U.S.C. § 1957(b)(2), which authorizes a fine equal to two times the amount of any criminally derived property involved in a money laundering transaction; 33 U.S.C. § 1319(c), which authorizes a fine of up to $50,000 per day for violations of the Water Pollution Control Act; 42 U.S.C. § 6928(d), which authorizes a fine of up to $50,000 per day for violations of the Resource Conservation Act; and 42 U.S.C. § 7413(c), which authorizes a fine of up to $25,000 per day for violations of the Clean Air Act.

6. The existence of income or assets that the defendant failed to disclose may justify a larger fine than that which otherwise would be warranted under §5E1.2. The court may base its conclusion as to this factor on information revealing significant unexplained expenditures by the defendant or unexplained possession of assets that do not comport with the defendant's reported income. If the court concludes that the defendant willfully misrepresented all or part of his income or assets, it may increase the offense level and resulting sentence in accordance with Chapter Three, Part C (Obstruction).

7. Subsection (i) provides for an additional fine sufficient to pay the costs of any imprisonment, probation, or supervised release ordered, subject to the defendant's ability to pay as prescribed in subsection (f). In making a determination as to the amount of any fine to be imposed under this provision, the court may be guided by reports published by the Bureau of Prisons and the Administrative Office of the United States Courts concerning average costs.

Index